NewMusicShelf

Anthology of New Music
Baritone, Vol. 1

Curated by Michael Kelly

Foreword by Libby Larsen

NewMusicShelf
www.newmusicshelf.com

NEWMUSICSHELF, INC.

Published in the United States of America
by NewMusicShelf, Inc.
34-29 32nd St., 3rd floor, Astoria, NY 11106
www.newmusicshelf.com

Copyright © 2018 by NewMusicShelf, Inc.

First printing 2018

All rights reserved. No part of this publication may be reproduced, stored in a retrieval system, or transmitted in any form or by any means, electronic, mechanical, photocopying, recording, or otherwise, without the prior permission of the publisher.

This anthology is dedicated to all who love song, who believe in the power of the combination of words and music, and who fill the air with their beautiful noises.

Contents

Acknowledgments vii
Foreword by Libby Larsen ix
Editor's Preface x
Introduction xi

Victoria Bond: Art and Science (2001) 1

Martin Bussey: Mr. Hancock's Letter (2010) 15
    from Garden Songs

D. Edward Davis: merman (2012) 24
    from two songs

Daniel Felsenfeld: You Want a Social Life, With Friends (2007) 29

Cara Haxo: Alone (2014) 39

Chia-Yu Hsu: Whispers of heavenly death (2000) 46

David Leisner: The Two Trees 51
    from O Love Is the Crooked Thing

Carrie Magin: Mnemosyne 62

Allen McCullough: The Happiest Day, The Happiest Hour (2004) 72
    from Edgar Allan Poe Song Cycle

Ryan Molloy: (Song of) Innisfail (2012) 80

Ben Moore: Love Remained (2011) 91
    from Love Remained

Gabrielle Rosse Owens: The Water is Wide (2016) 98
    from Three Folk Songs

Paul Salerni: Alley Cat Love Song (2007) 103
from Bad Pets

Harry Stafylakis: This Living Hand (2007) 113
from The Keats Cycle

Margaret Tesch-Muller: There is a Solemn Wind Tonight (2016) 118
from Voices of a Northern Year

Craig Urquhart: Among the Multitude (1980) 126
from Leaves

Mark Lanz Weiser: Looking Back at Spring (2001) 129

Philip Wharton: Rum Tum Tiddy-Um (2011) 150
from Blooms Remembered

Scott Wheeler: Commuter Buddhist (2014) 160

David Wolfson: Pizza or Chinese (2015) 167
from The Ballad of Unintended Consequences

About the Curator 173
About the Composes 174
Supplemental Materials 194

FOREWORD

Congratulations! You hold in your hands the *NewMusicShelf Anthologies of New Music*, a four-volume, curated treasure trove of 80 songs penned by your colleague composers and composed for you, singer of songs, teller of tales, bearer of our zeitgeist. Discover and prize these songs. They are yours now, in your keeping, waiting to rise on your breath and sing through your voices.

You might think of these four volumes of song as living-history - a vibrant mix of singers, collaborative instrumentalists, composers and our audiences. A wide range of the many excellent composers writing art song today are represented here. They are a community of composers who love the human voice and devote their talent and time to composing new work for it. We honor these composers through performance, of course, by singing the songs they write for us. We also must remind ourselves that we need to honor their work by respecting their need to support themselves with compensation in the form of the royalties they collect from sales of their music. We urge you to support your composers by resisting the temptation to photocopy and distribute music from these song collections. As the world becomes more and more digital, we think it essential that these collections of songs are available only in print. In the years to come we will be delighted to discover the *NewMusicShelf Anthologies of New Music* on pianos, bookshelves and music stands, but even more delighted to hear you filling the air with the sound of your singing - these songs - everywhere!

— Libby Larsen

Acknowledgments

Thank you...

...Dennis Tobenski for this incredible idea, and for bringing me on board with Laura Dixon Strickling and Megan Ihnen. The dream team! Thank you all for your wisdom, ideas, and collaboration in making this crazy project come to life.

...Jean Barr, for making me aware of my gifts and inspiring me to forge forward.
...Margo Garrett, for inspiring me to walk through the world of song with confidence, armed with great knowledge.
...Kathy Kelly, my brilliant and ever-inspiring creative partner for being so dedicated to our music making. You keep me honest, and you give me wings… all at once.
...Libby Larsen, for your brain and your heart and your craft.
...Isabel Leonard, for being a soundboard for my ideas and always giving me good advice.
...Shannon McGinnis, we met and so did our minds. Thank you for saying yes to so many things.
...Ben Moore, for making my dream come true of having my words set to music.
...William Norris, for putting up with me on the couch, surrounded by paper, my headphones in and completely unresponsive… for months.
...Paul Sperry and Joy In Singing, for recognizing and celebrating my love of this art form.
...Brian Zeger, for sharpening my critical thinking and expanding my awareness of what song could be.

...My brother, Chris, for showing me what dedication looks like.
...My mother, for being my champion and my number one fan.

And a very special thank you to all of the amazing composers, both included in this volume and those that submitted for consideration. Your talent and vision infuse this art form with life and secure it as an exciting and ever-changing place to work and create. Keep making new songs for the world to hear.

— Michael Kelly

Editor's Preface

This volume - and series of publications - exists to introduce performing musicians to the amazing variety of composers living and writing today. Whether you're a student, teacher, or professional, this collection was created with you in mind.

Every song is appropriate for a professional or student recital, and many songs were selected for their didactic possibilities: shifting meters, asymmetrical rhythms, various degrees of difficulty with pitch materials or non-traditional performance techniques, etc.

Across all four inaugural volumes of these anthologies, the primary criterion has been the curator's willingness to stand behind their selections: to be willing to perform and record every song, and make their selections without reservation. These are songs that singers should *know*, and should perform. These are composers that singers should *know*, and should work with.

And *you* are performers that composers should get to know and work with! We are all a part of a community that makes music, and we can only be better and stronger together.

As the creator of this series, I've had to personally define my short-, medium-, and long-term goals for the project. My short-term goal is simple: you getting to know these songs, and performing them. I stand behind every song and every composer, and hope that you find your own connection to these songs.

My medium-term goal is linked to a minor feature of these volumes: notice that underneath many of the song titles there is a bit of text: "from _____". Many of these songs are from song cycles or song sets. I encourage you to check out those cycles, as well as the composer's other vocal works! My medium-term goal? That you and your colleagues get to know more of the works by these composers than are represented here. This is a mere sliver of these composers' output, and their catalogs are worth exploring!

My long-term goal? Let's just say that I have plans....

I encourage you to look beyond the borders of the voice-type specific nature of these volumes. Many of these songs were written without gender or voice type in mind, and so are worth exploring by every singer.

— Dennis Tobenski
Founder of NewMusicShelf

Introduction

It's not every day that we discover a piece of music that sets us on a journey of inspiration. There are a myriad of brilliant songs to discover in the world, but finding them isn't always as simple as it may seem. I've spent many years in pursuit of songs to populate specific moments in a recital program that capture an exact emotion, attitude, idea, or concept. I've made a career out of building interesting and thought-provoking programs, but what has driven me the most is the thrill of searching for a song that ignites my imagination. Nothing is more satisfying than that moment of awakening you feel upon hearing it for the first time. I present this volume of songs to you in that spirit of discovery. They are yours to cherish and to choose from for your own recitals. My hope is that one (or many) of these songs will be a spark for your brilliant programming ideas.

To me, the most exciting reward of all is that this collection connects you to an interesting and varied collection of living, active composers. You may be familiar with some of them already. Most likely, though, you will have never heard the songs included in this anthology. In fact, I was unaware of many of them before we began the selection process. Their music is clearly inspired by the historic repertoire of the great masters of song composition. However, here we find songs born of their own unique and modern artistic voices. I have no doubt they will one day be considered historic masters themselves. You will be delighted to find that the poetry they have set runs the gamut of styles and themes from humor to heartache, and everything in between.

These composers and their work give me much confidence in the vibrancy of the art of song. It is alive and thrives in their imaginative compositions. All it awaits is the addition of the nuanced colors of your artistry. These songs, and the multitude of others that have been written are at your artistic disposal. I invite you to be wildly creative in finding new and exciting ways to present them. This volume can stand as a mere springboard for your searches, and kindling for your imagination. So discover well, perform often, and continue the great tradition of this venerable art form.

— Michael Kelly

To Stephan, my Einstein
Art and Science

ALBERT EINSTEN

VICTORIA BOND
(2001)

Music copyright © Protone Music 2001.
Text by Albert Einstein (1921); used with permission from The Albert Einstein Archives, The Hebrew University of Jerusalem.

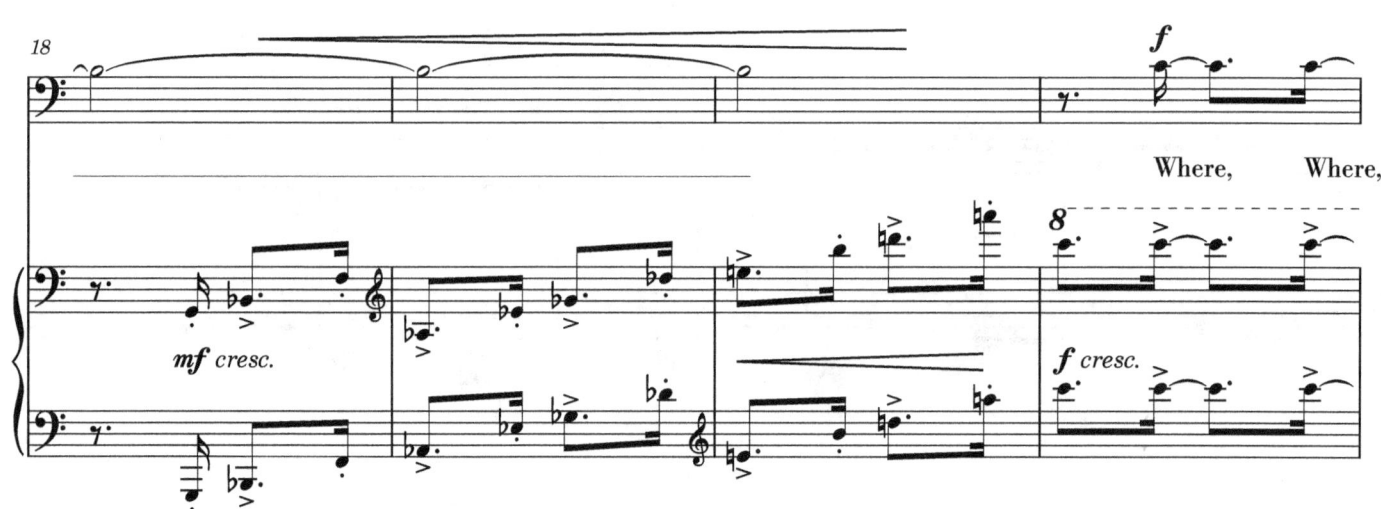

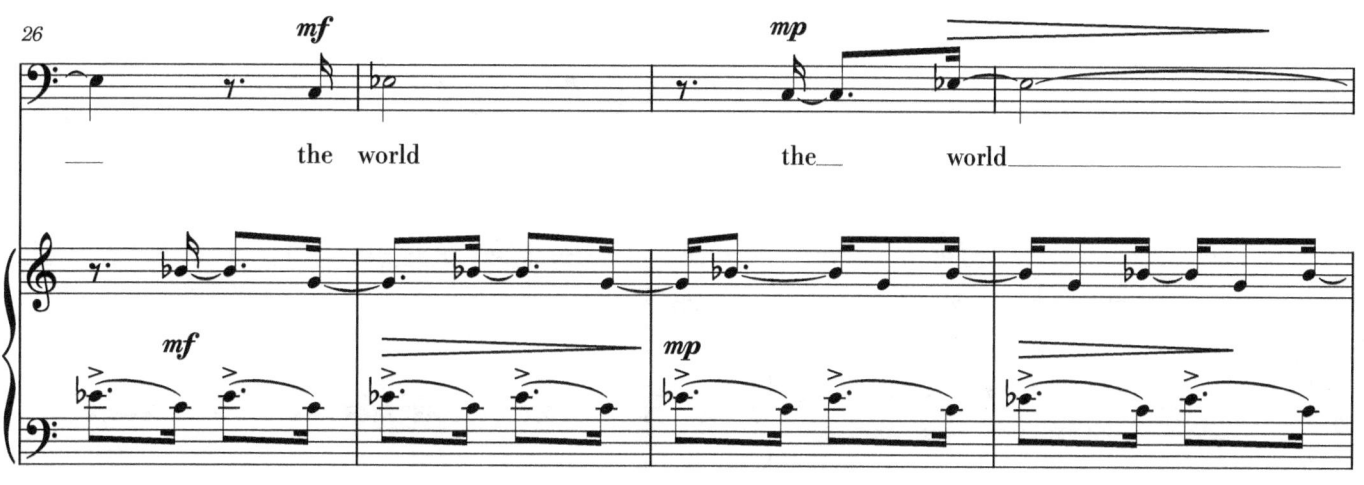

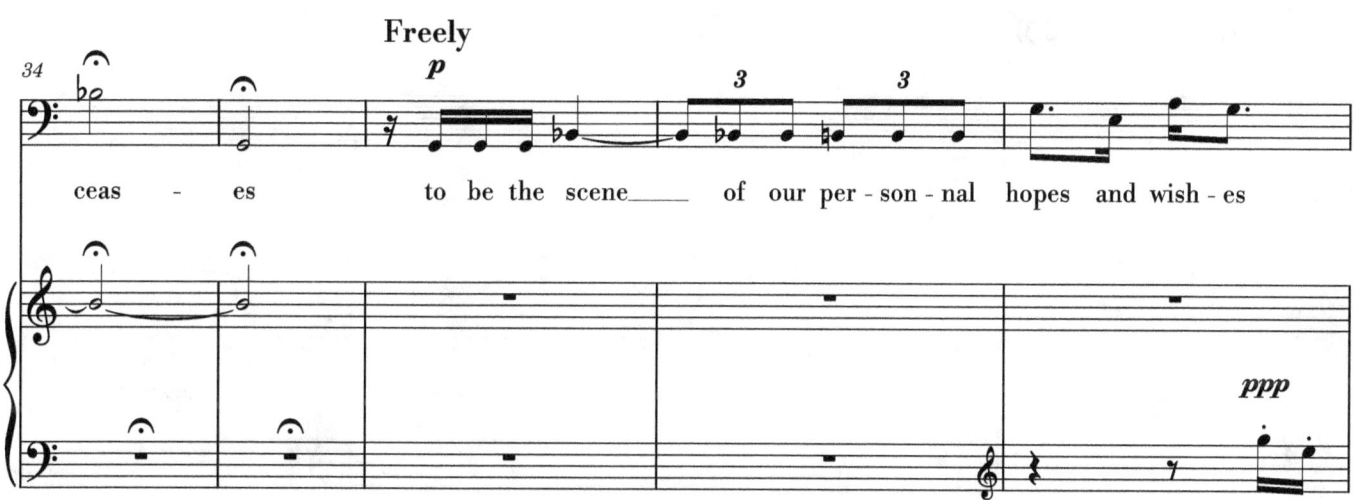

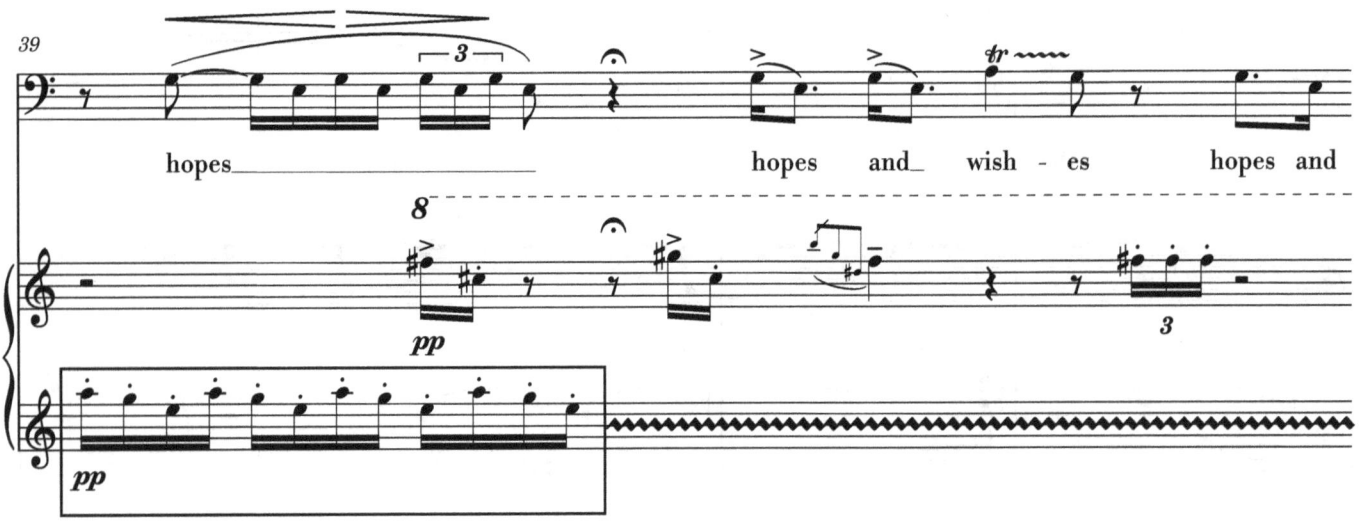

Gently flowing (♩. = 60)

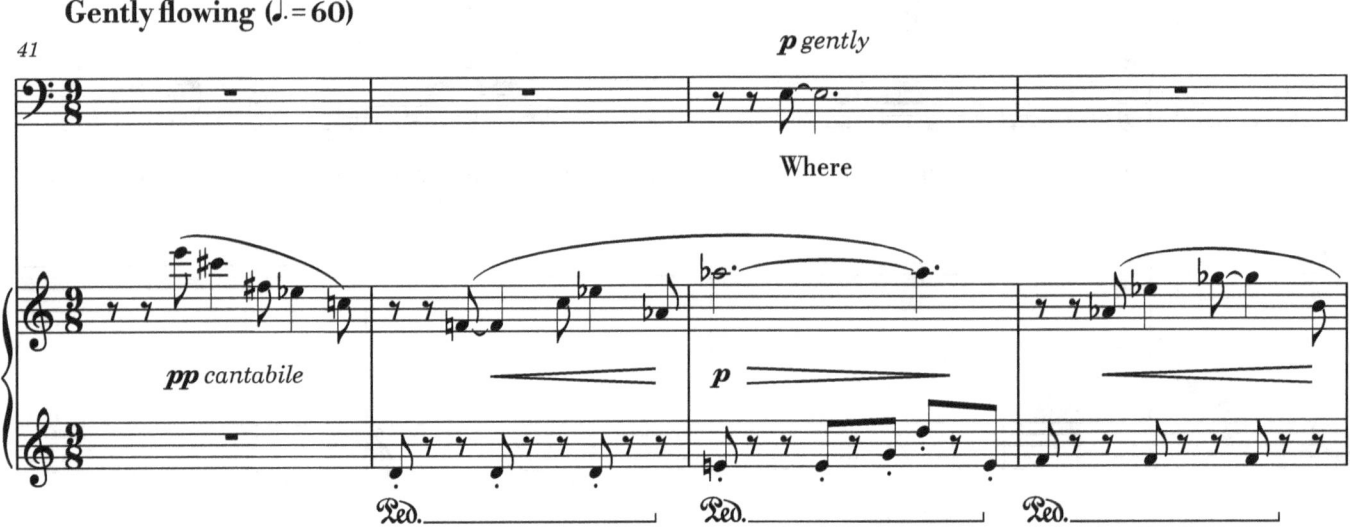

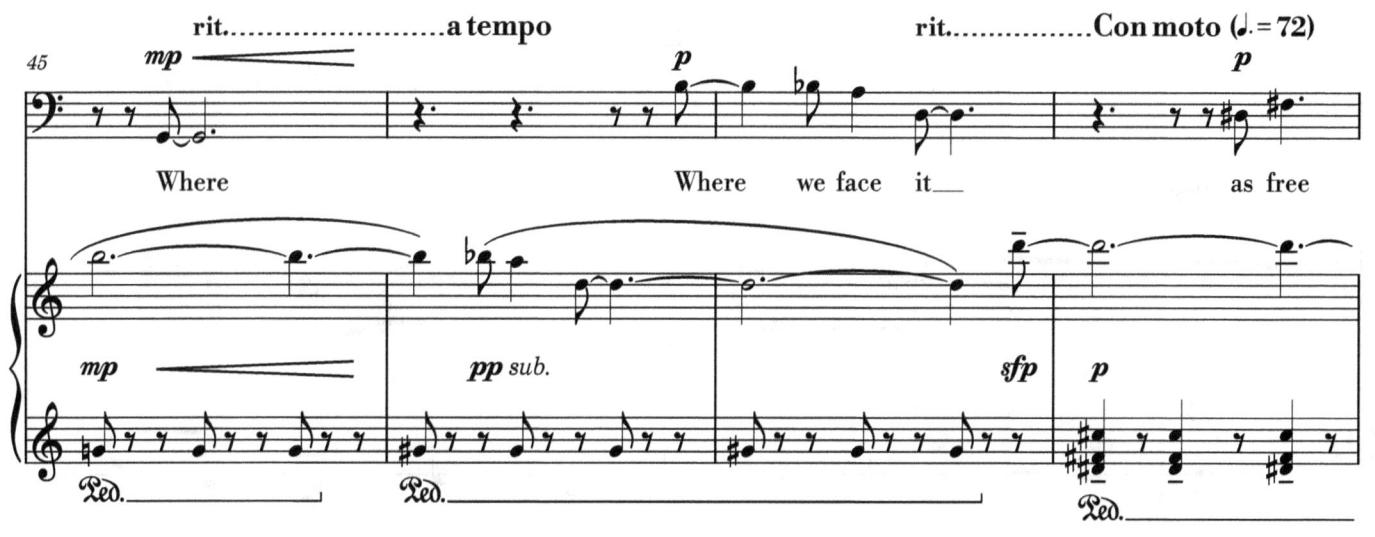

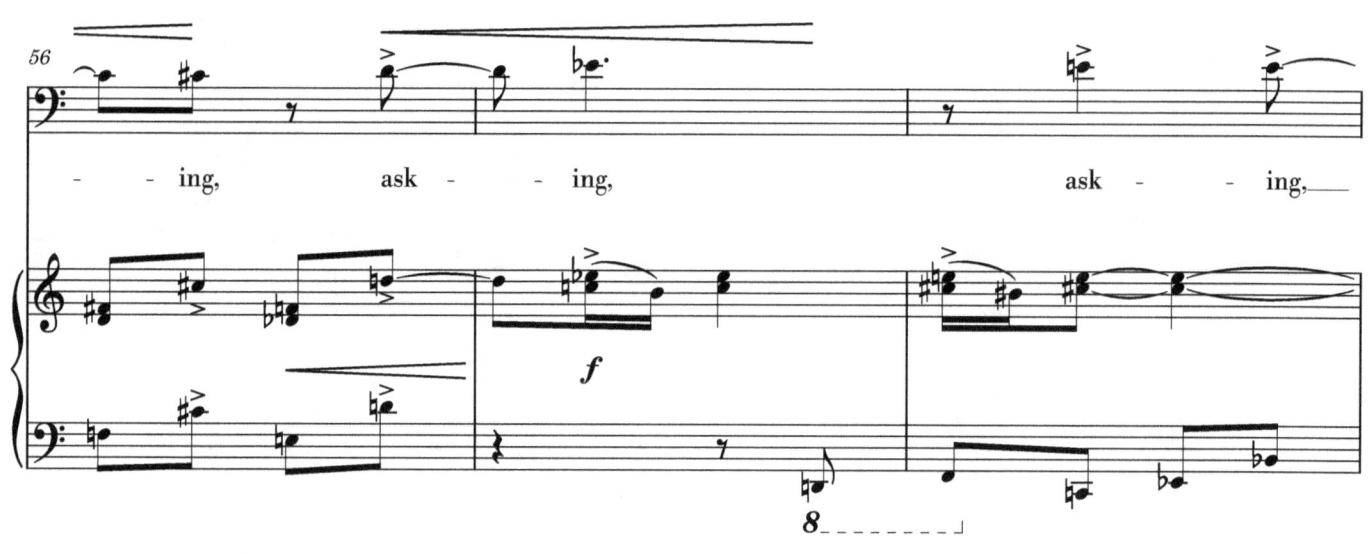

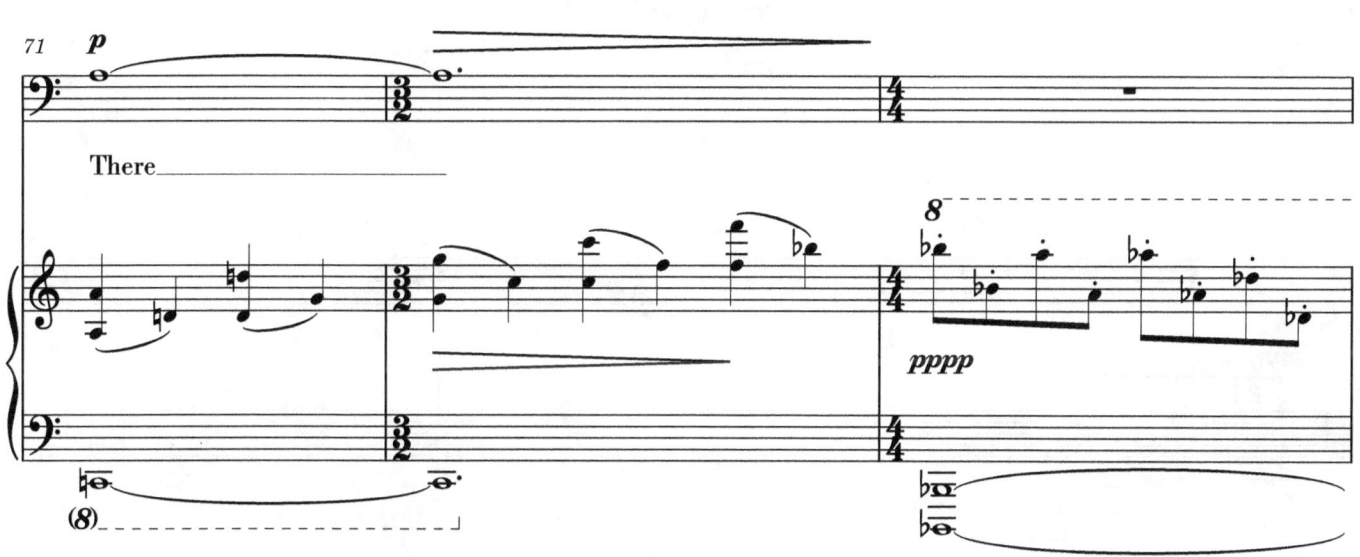

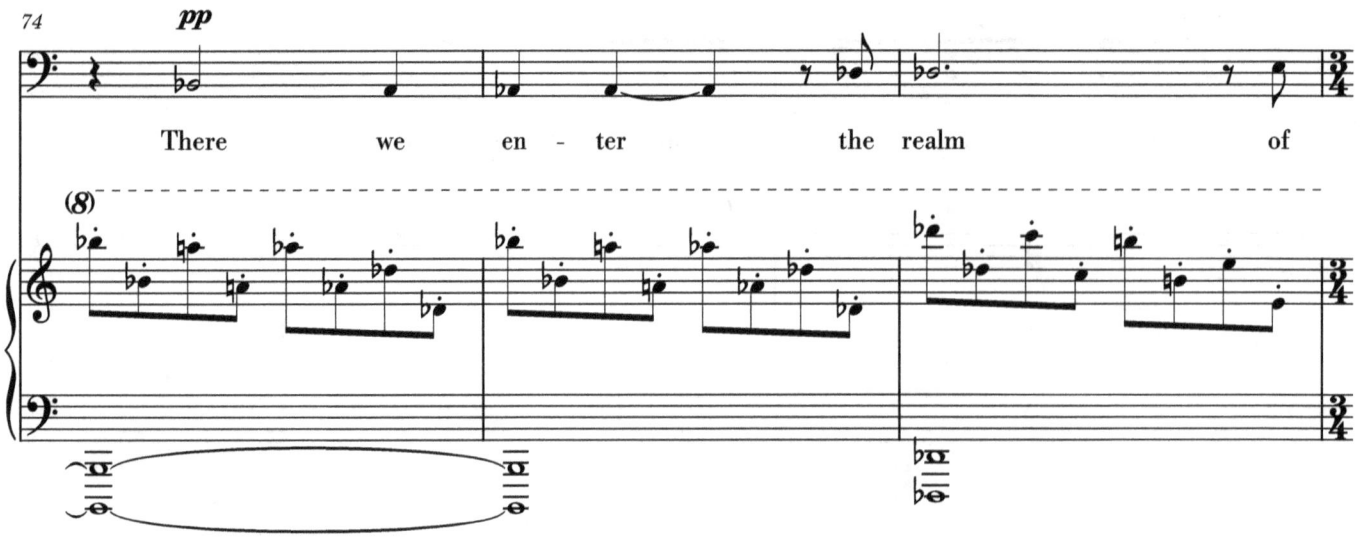

Allegro agitato (♩=128)

Adagio misterioso (♩=44)

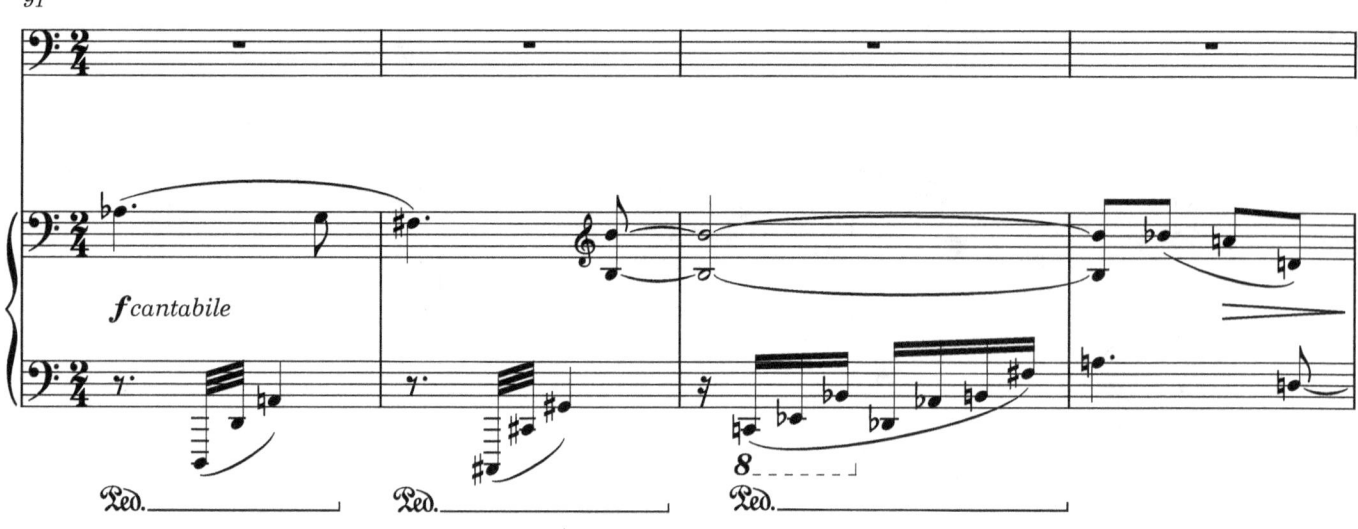

If it is com-mu-ni-cat-ed

voice without strict rhythm, independent of the piano

through forms whose con-nec-tions are not ac-cess-i-ble

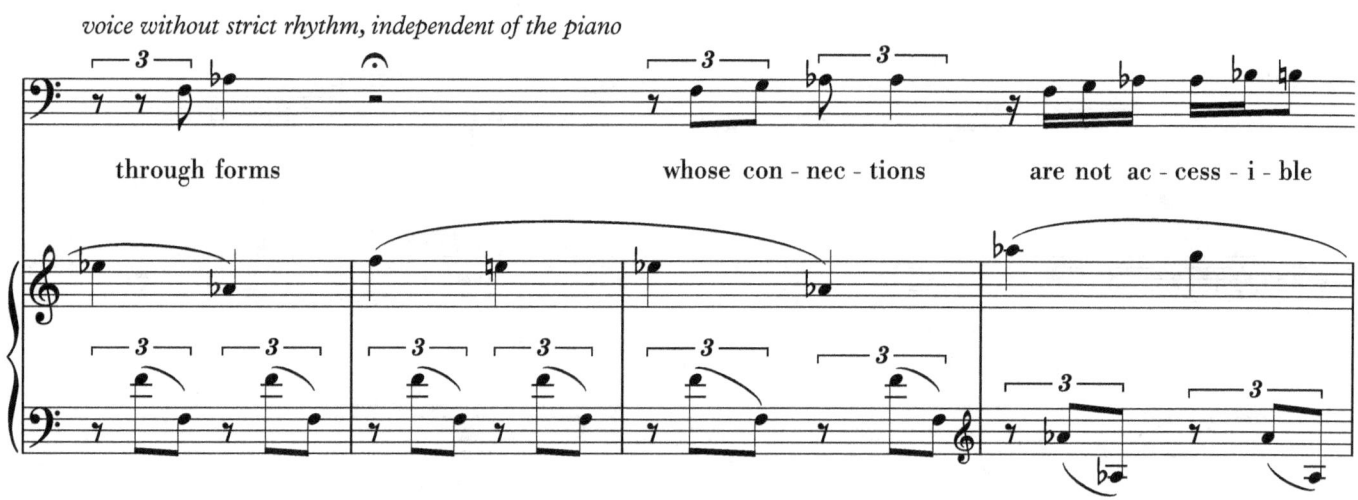

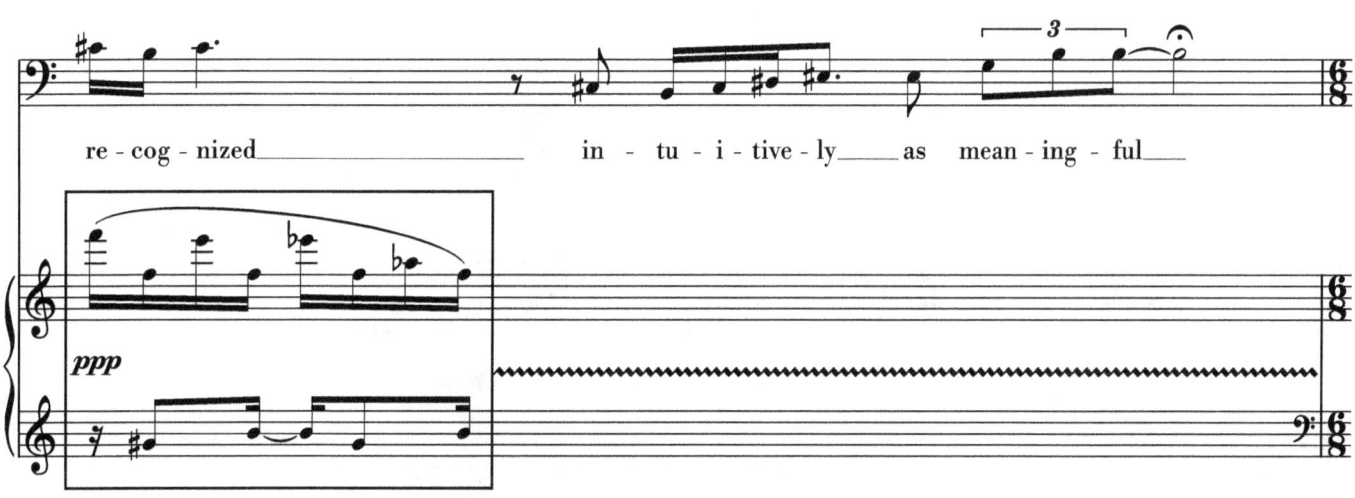
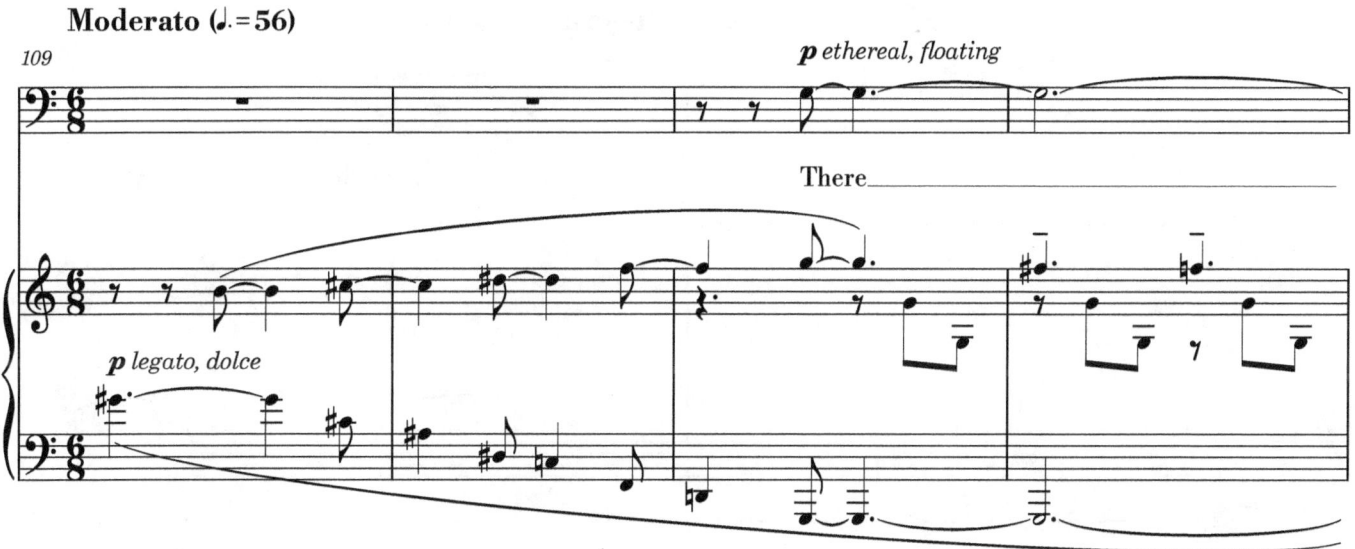

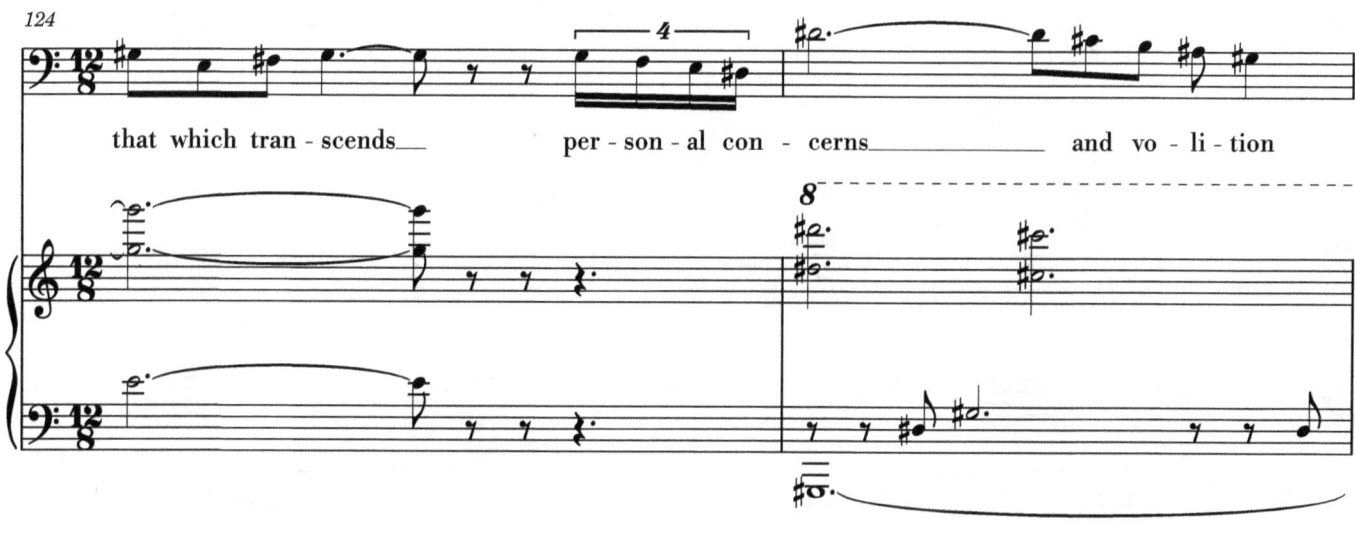

Mr. Hancock's Letter

from Garden Songs

THOMAS HANCOCK

MARTIN BUSSEY
(2010)

Copyright © Martin Bussey

17

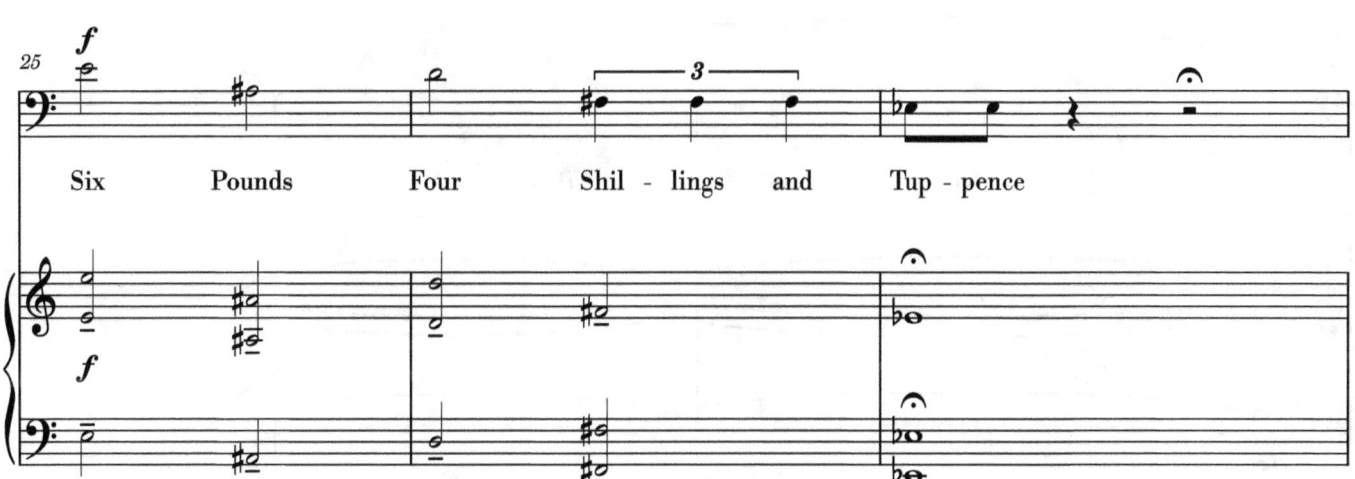

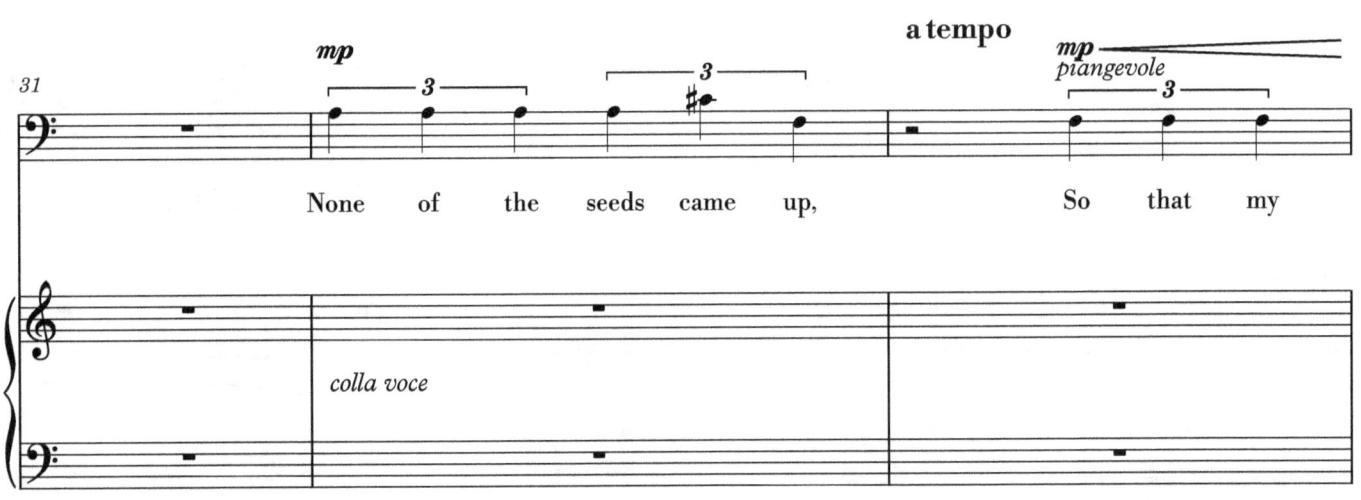
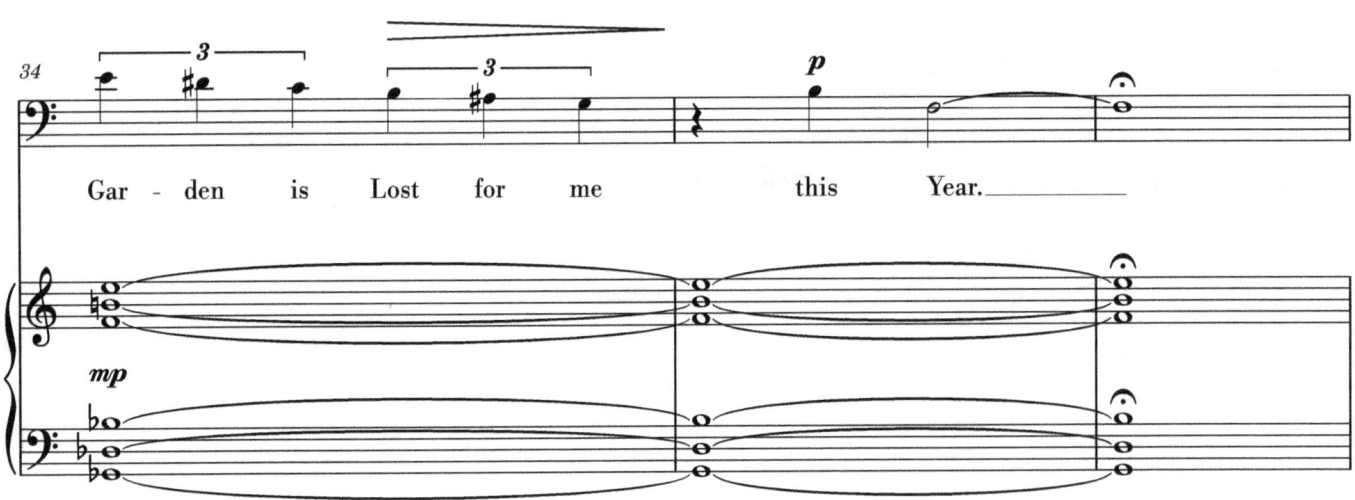

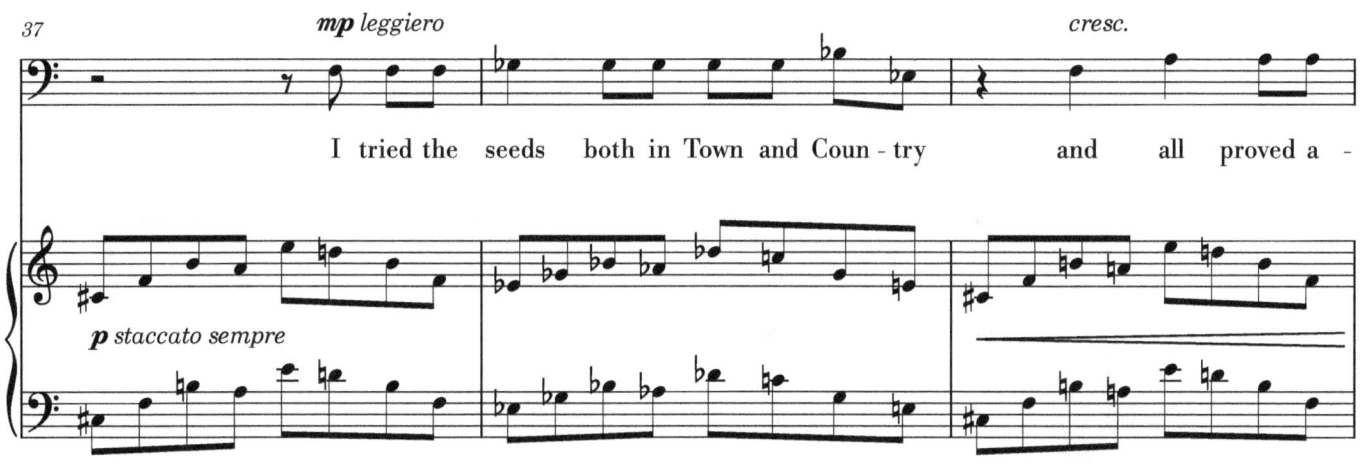
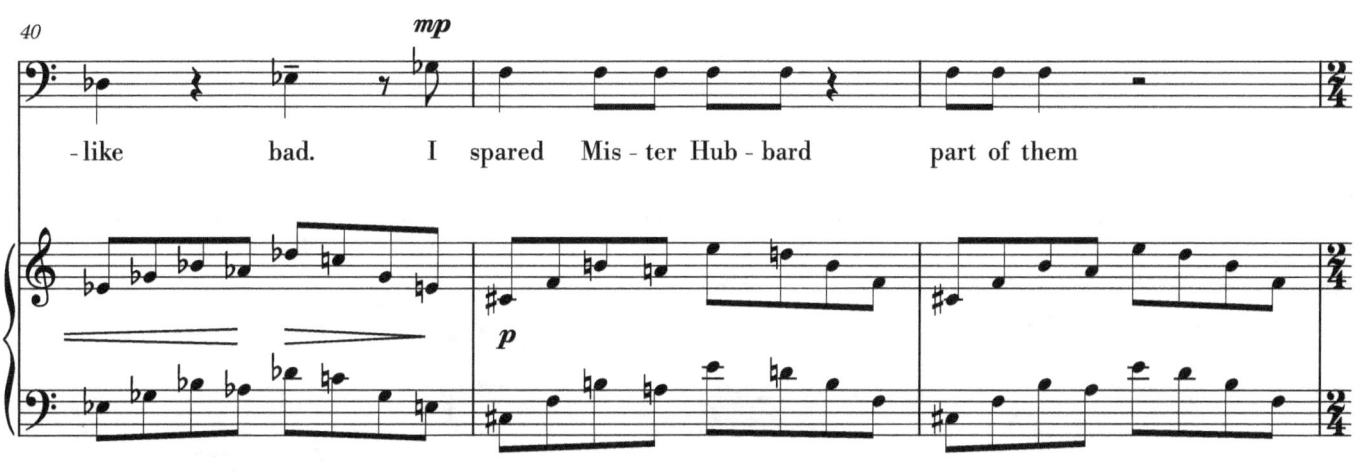

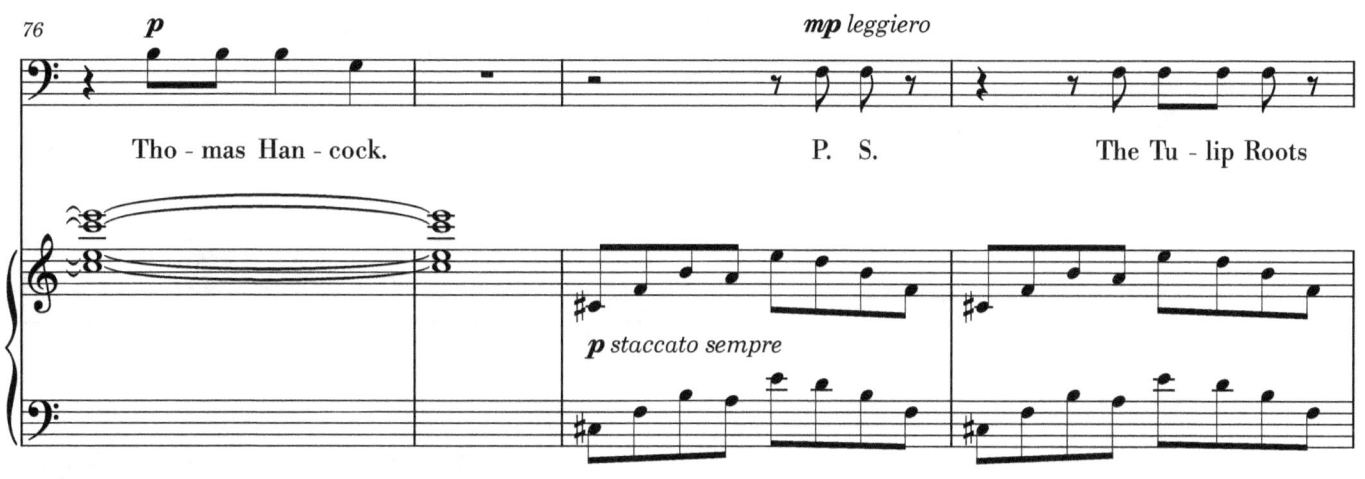

merman
from two songs

GERARD WOZEK

D. EDWARD DAVIS
(2012)

Copyright © 2012 by D. Edward Davis and Gerard Wozek. All Rights Reserved.

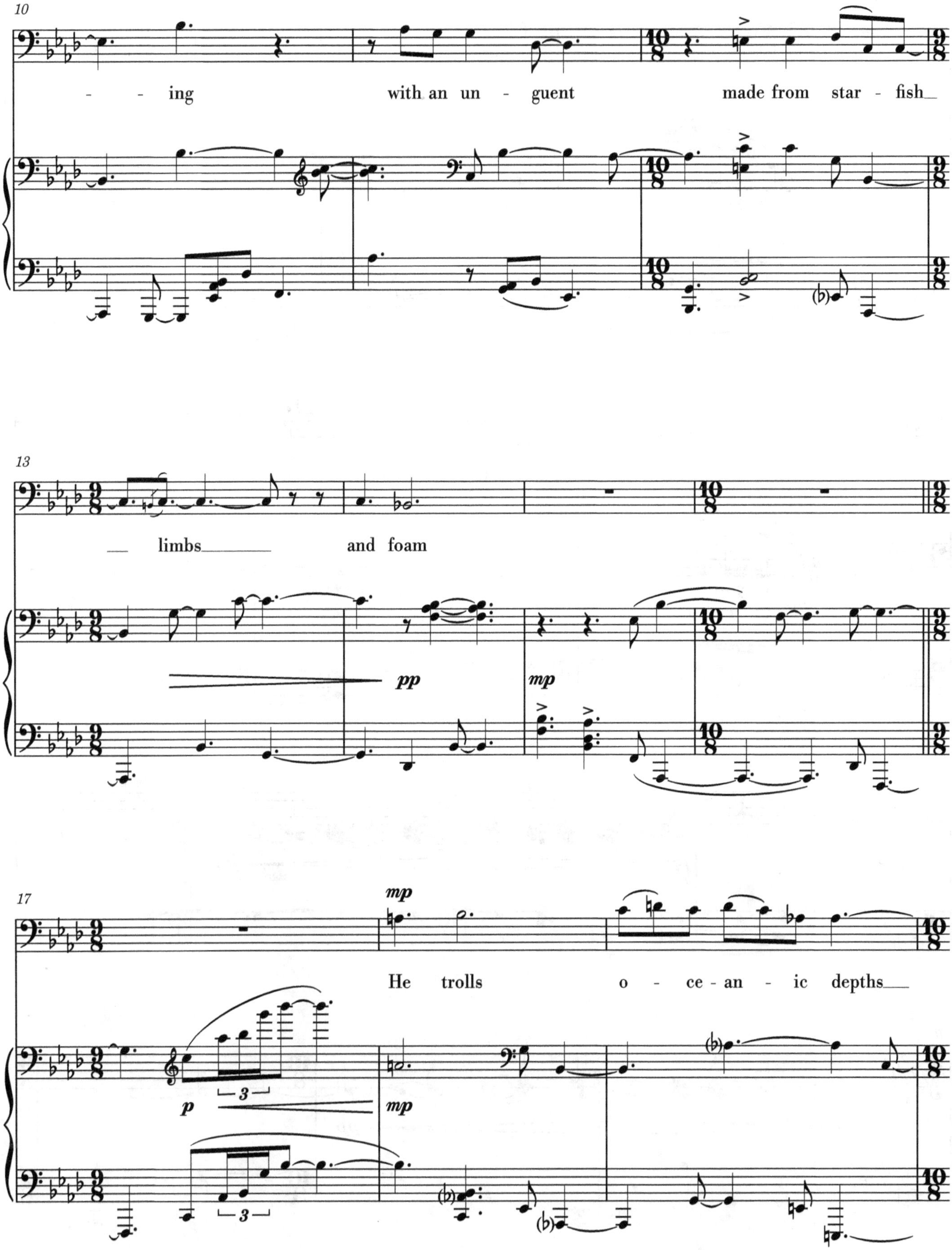
10
- - ing with an un - guent made from star - fish
13
limbs and foam
pp
mp
17
mp
He trolls o - ce - an - ic depths
p
mp

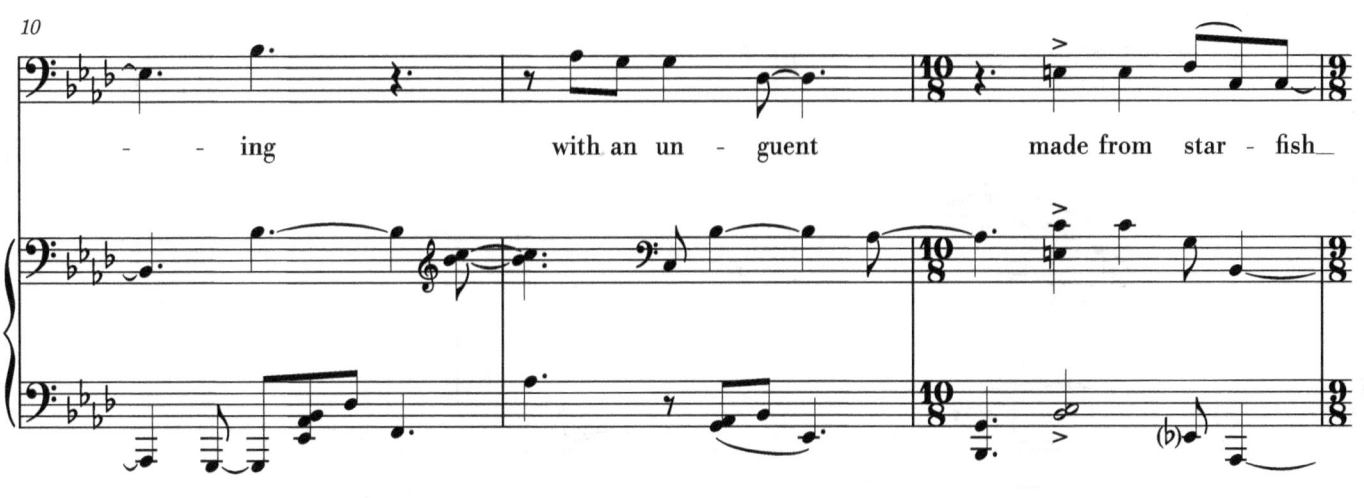

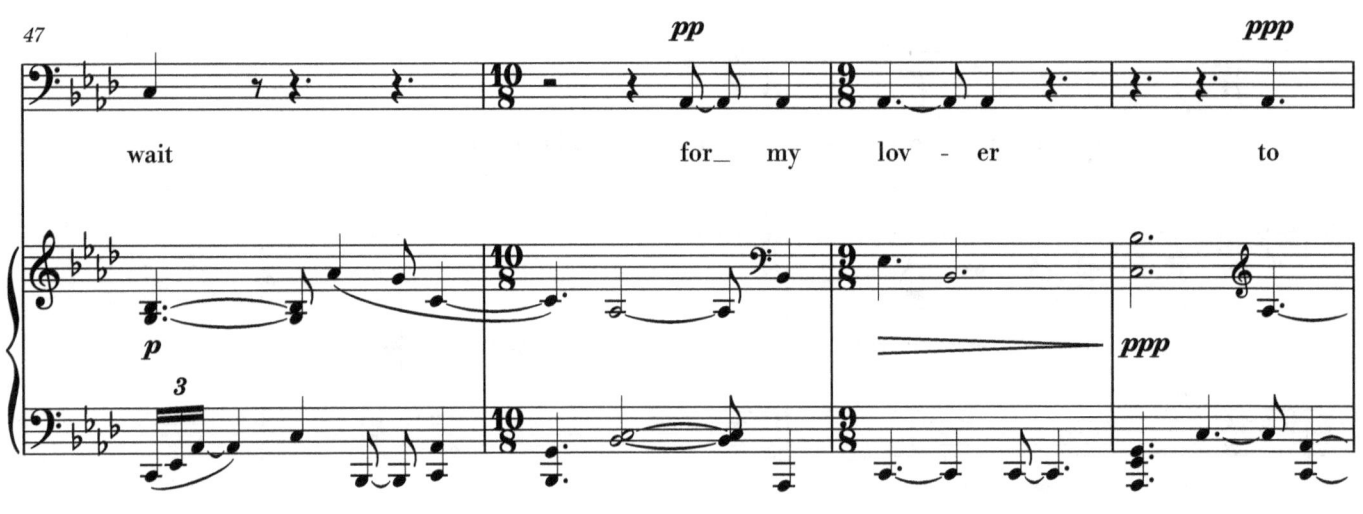

for Matthew Worth
You Want a Social Life, With Friends

KENNETH KOCH DANIEL FELSENFELD
(2007)

Copyright © 2007 Felsenmusick Publishing Concern

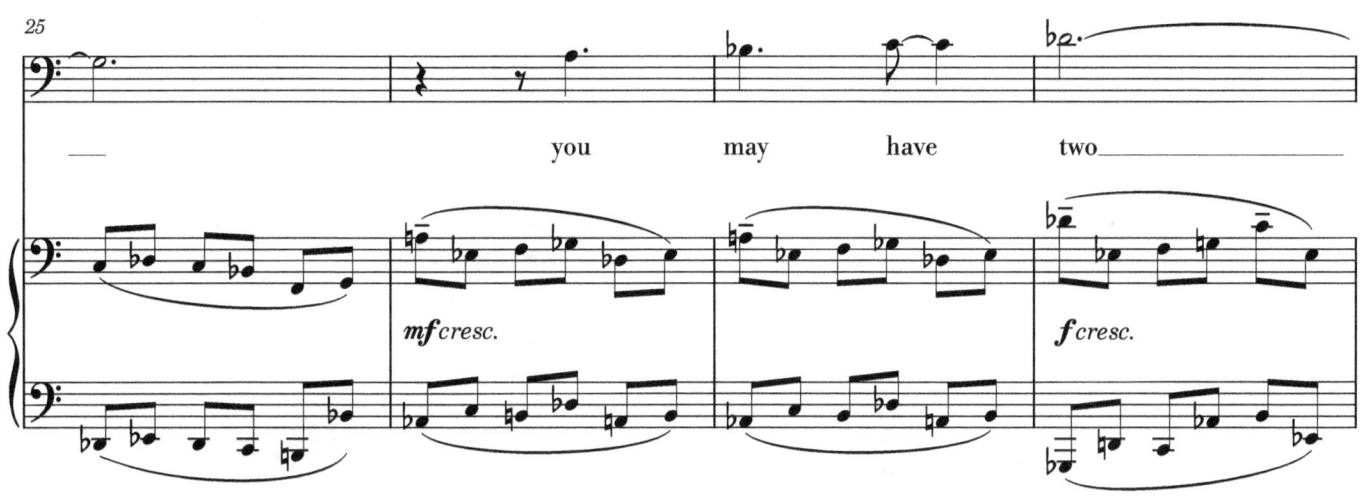
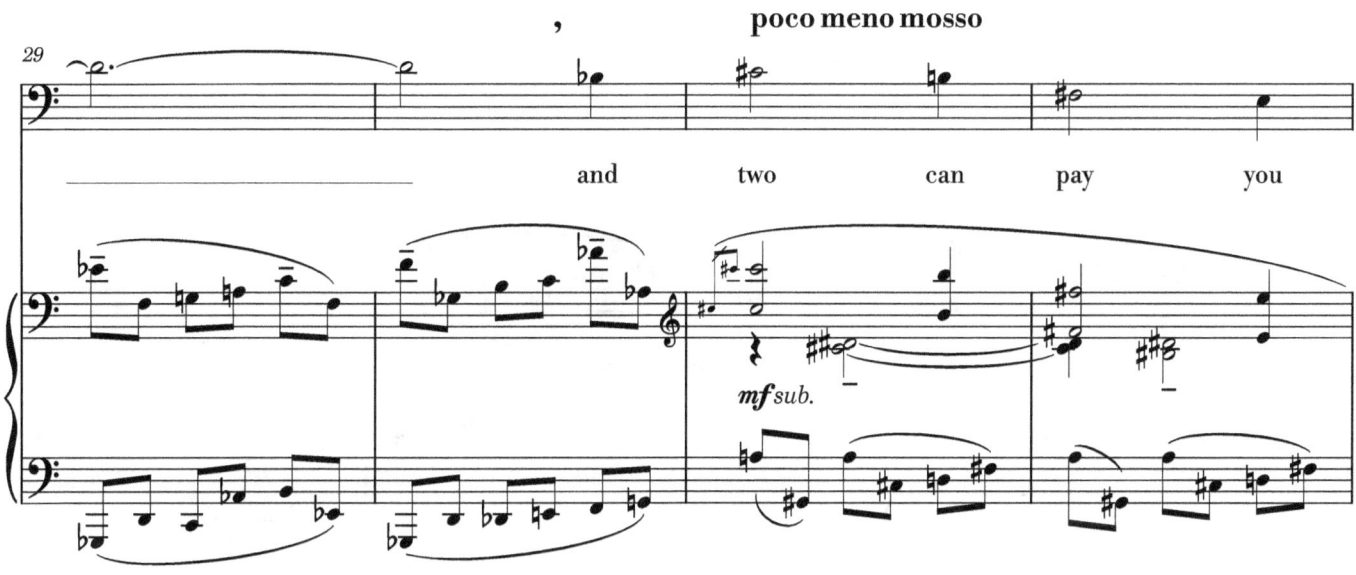

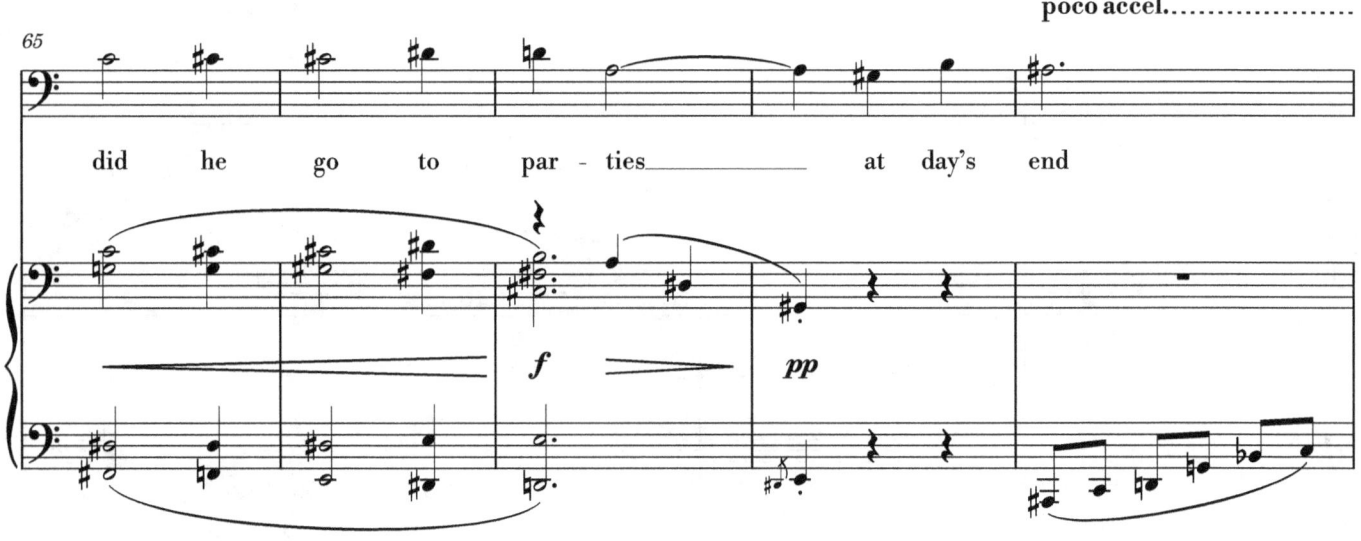
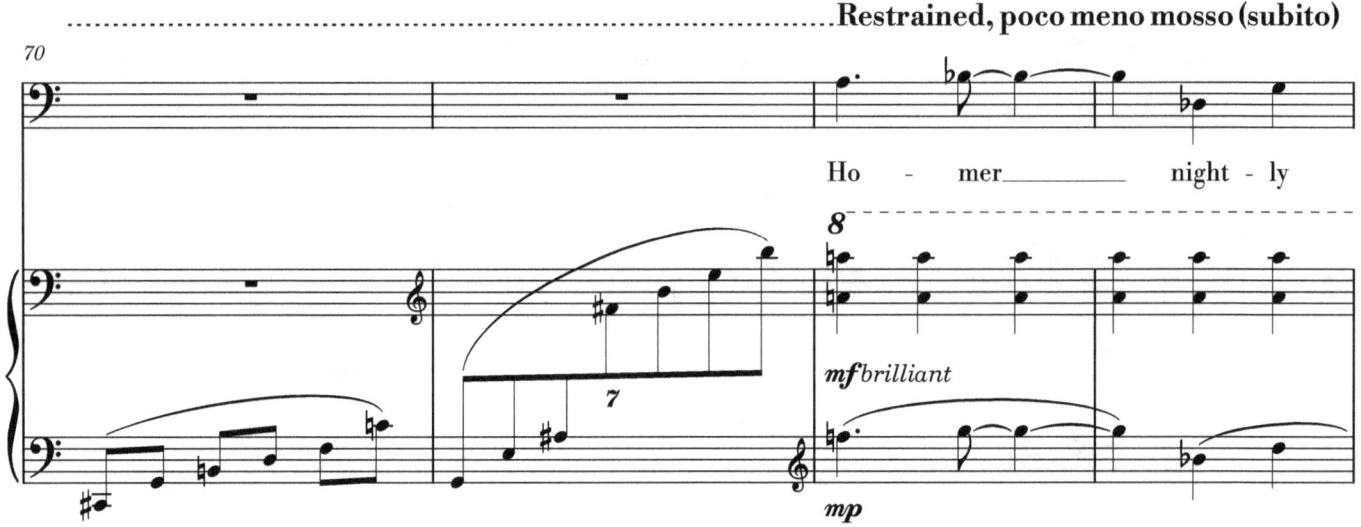

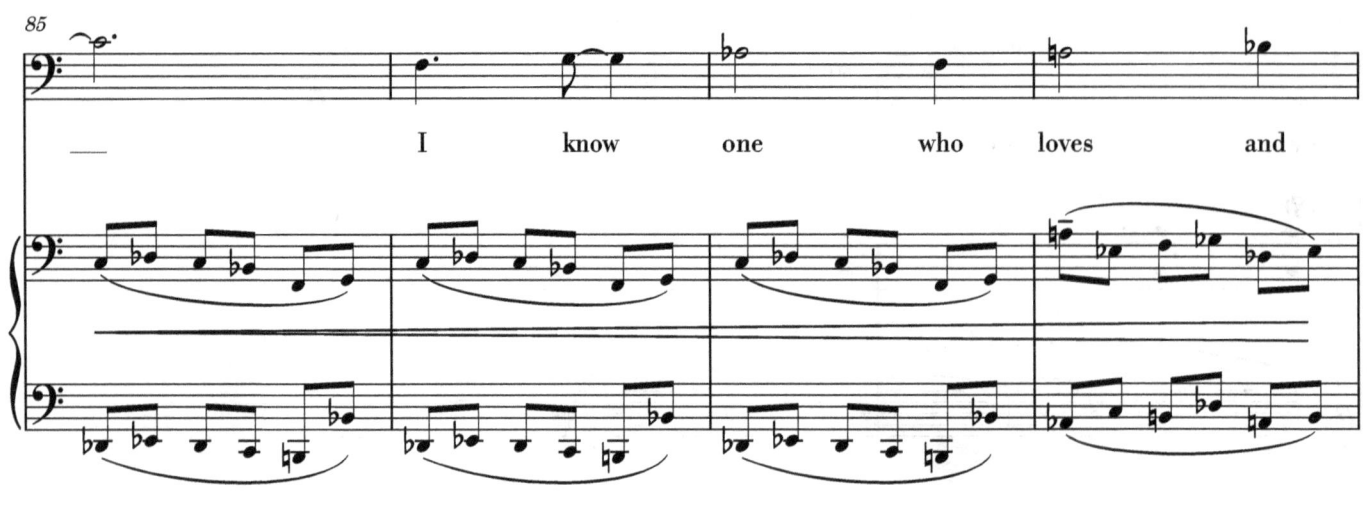
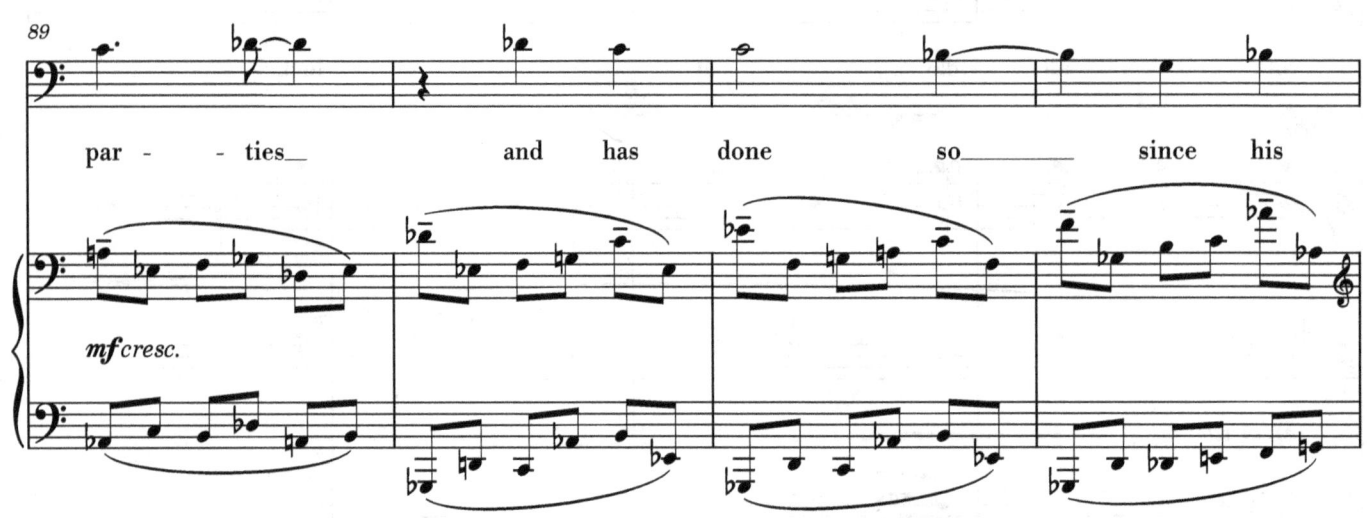

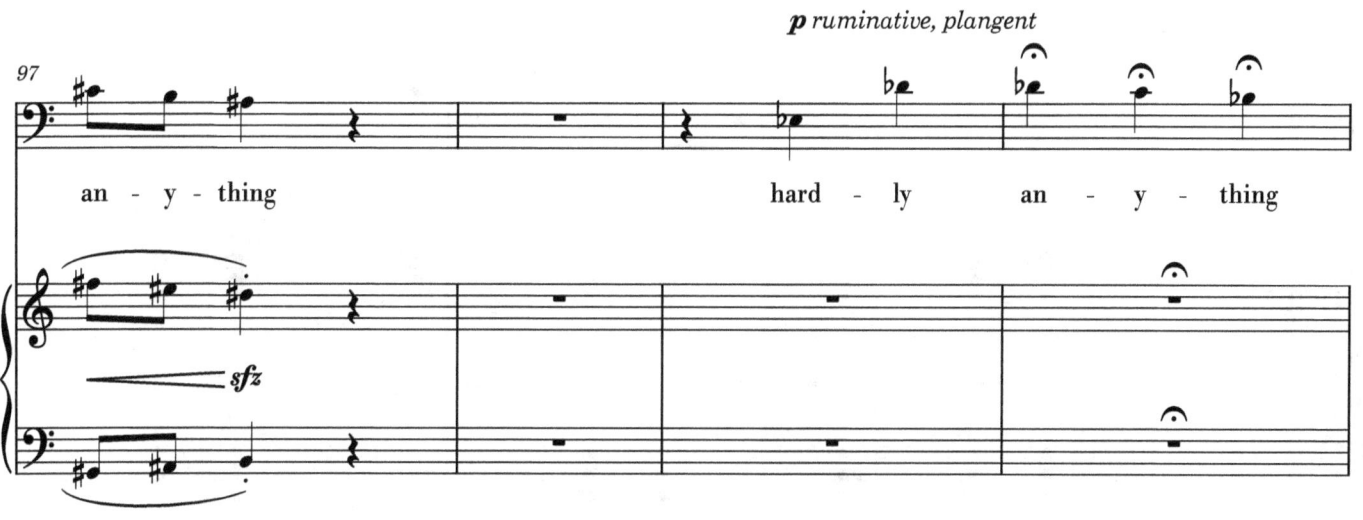
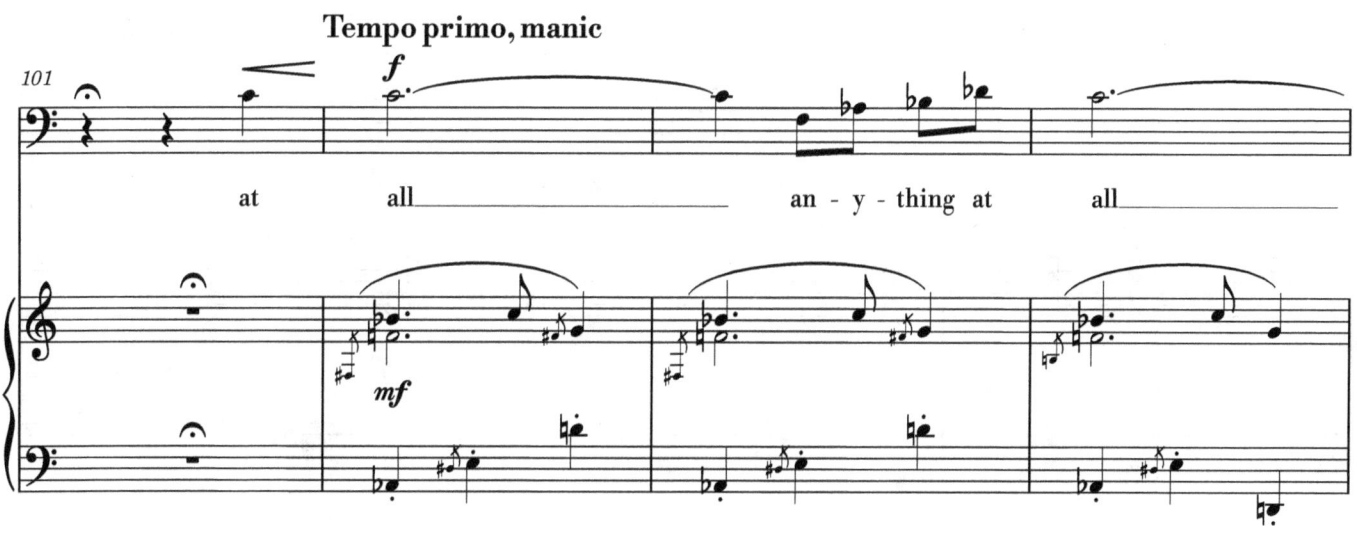

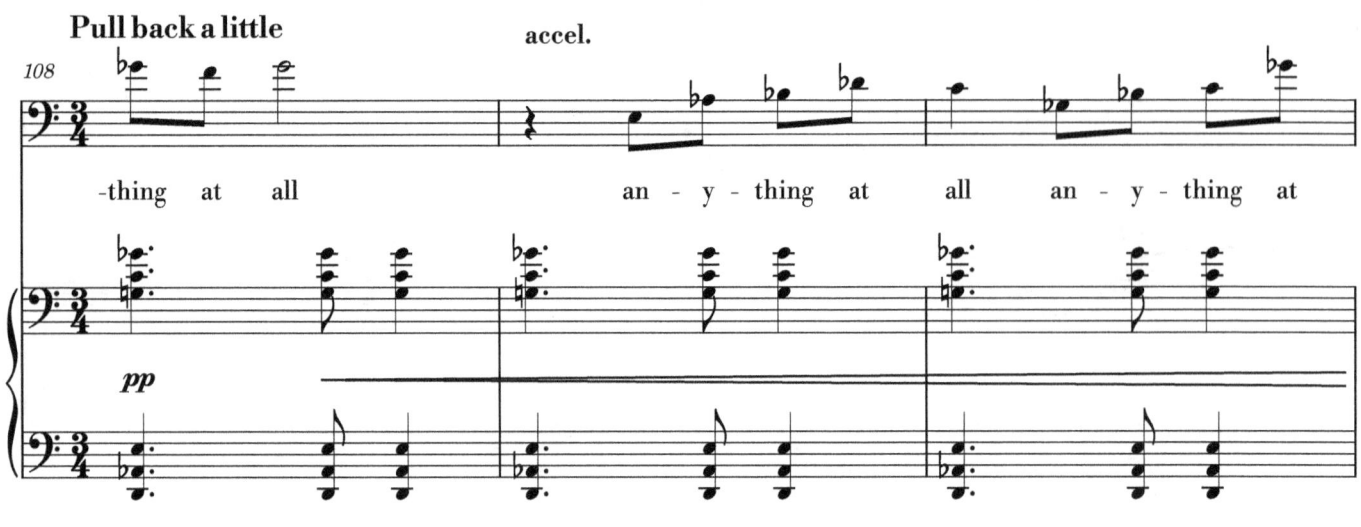

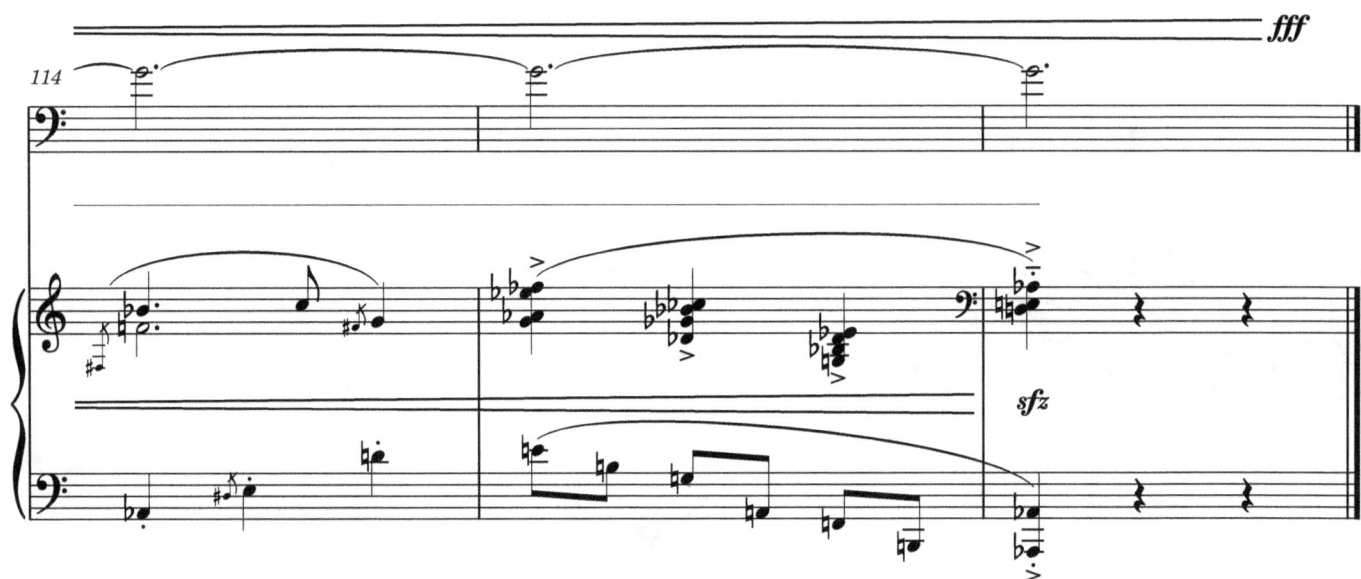

Alone

EDGAR ALLAN POE

CARA HAXO
(2014)

Copyright © 2014 by Cara Haxo. All Rights Reserved.

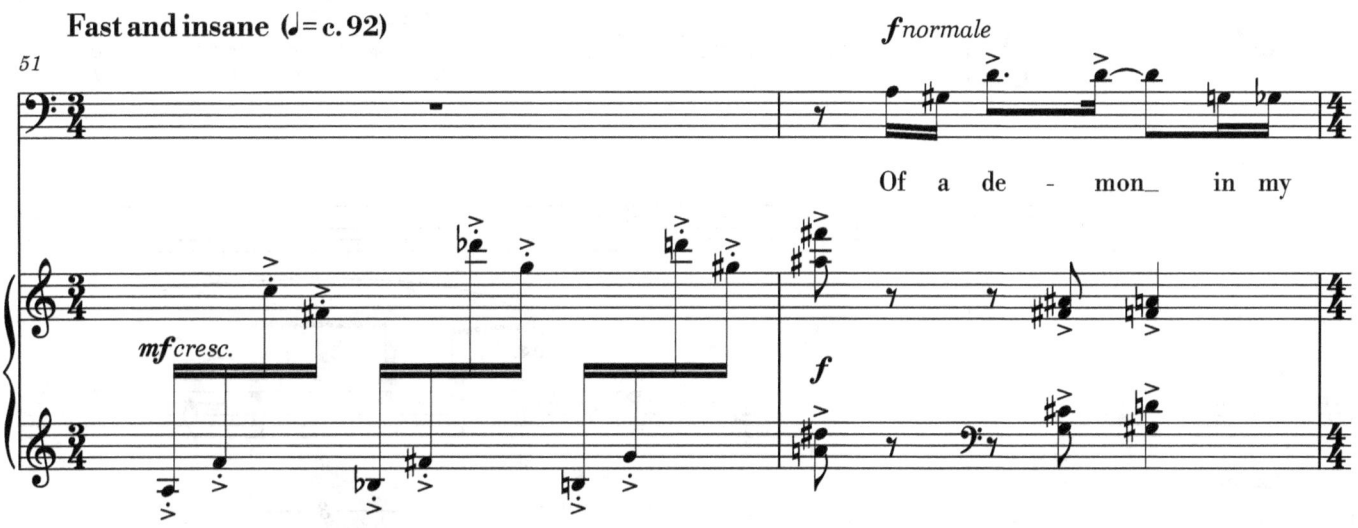

Whispers of heavenly death

WALT WHITMAN

CHIA-YU HSU
(2000)

Calme (♩= 46–52)

Copyright © 2000 by Chia-Yu Hsu

48

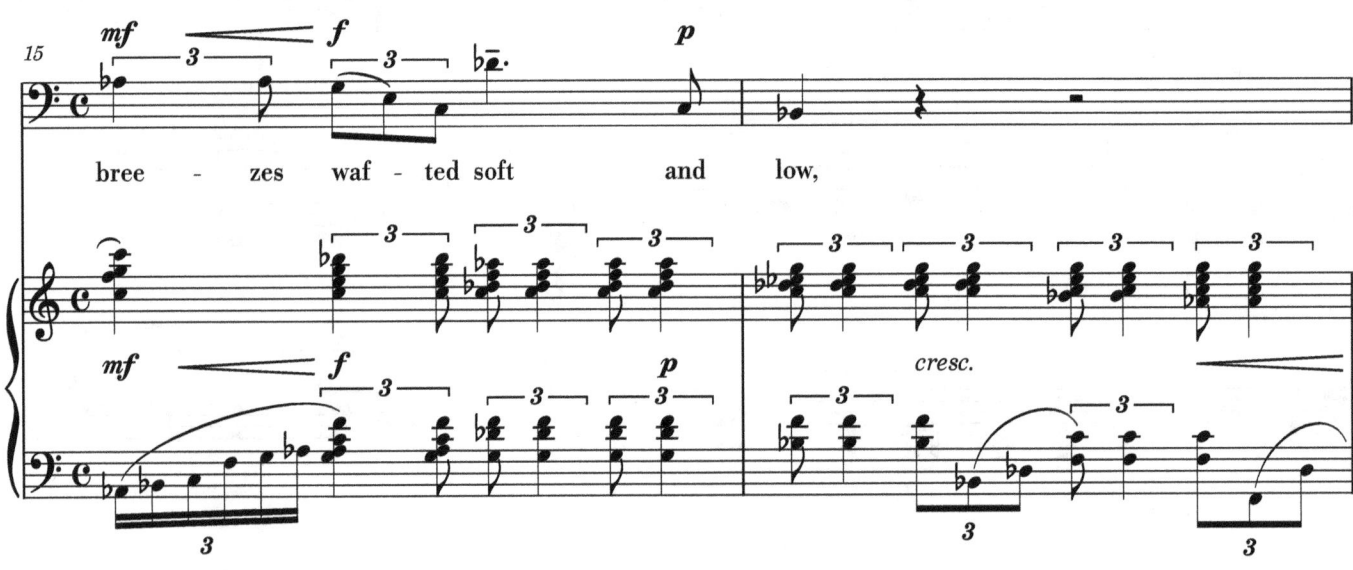

The Two Trees
from O Love Is the Crooked Thing

WILLIAM BUTLER YEATS

DAVID LEISNER
(1980)

Copyright © 2010 by Merion Music, Inc. All Rights Reserved.
International Copyright Secured.

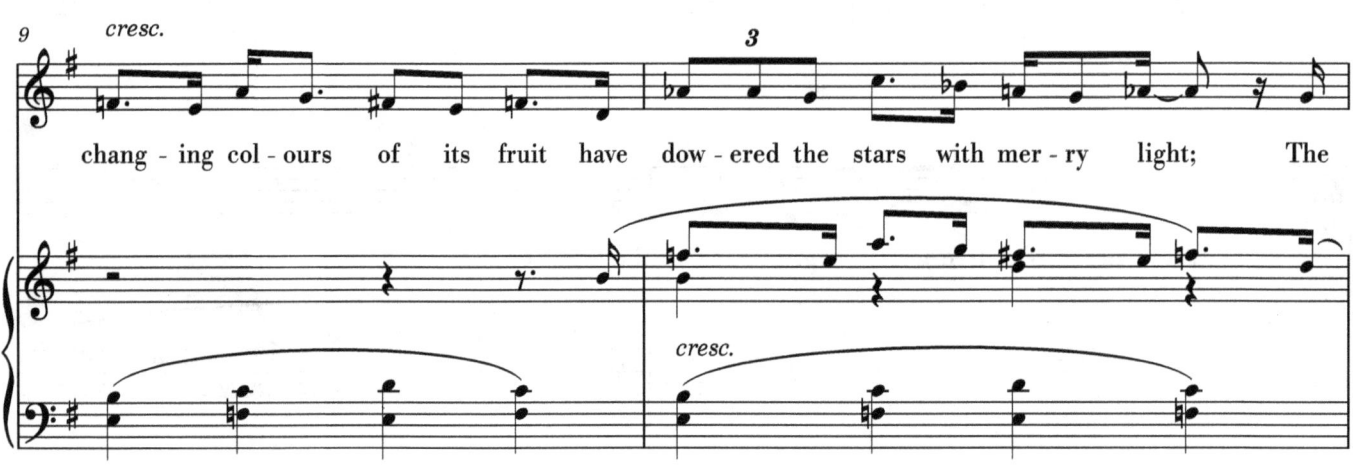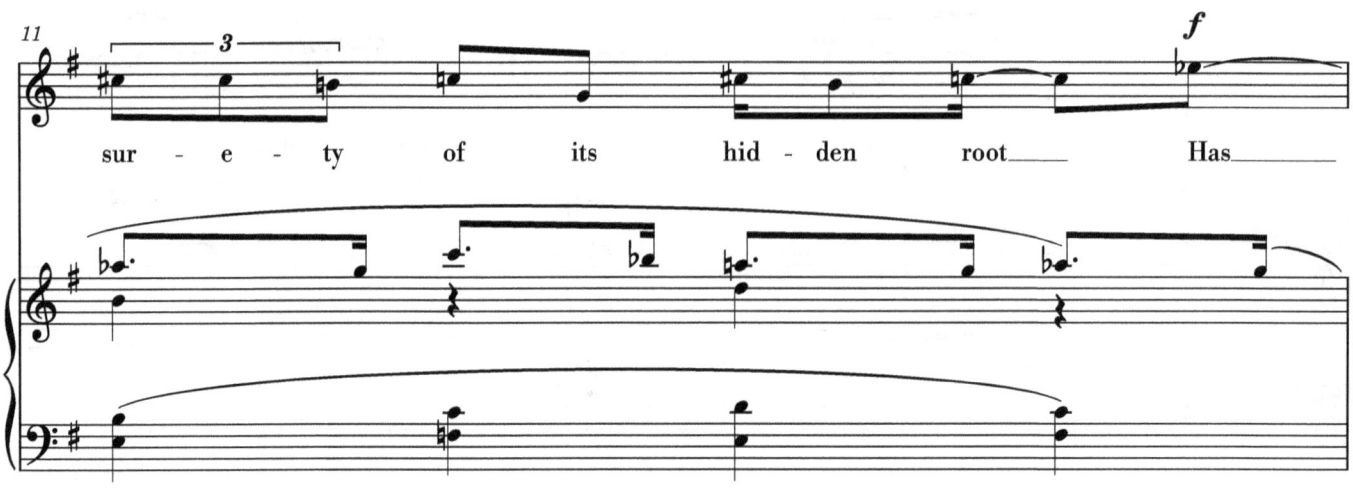

54

*All grace notes occur before the beat

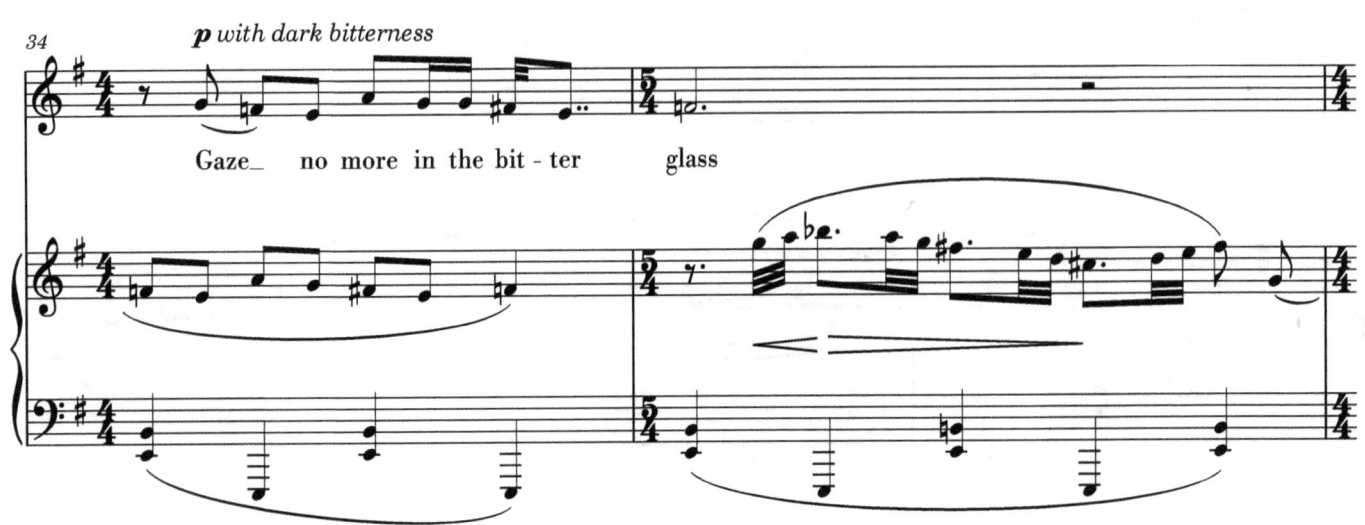

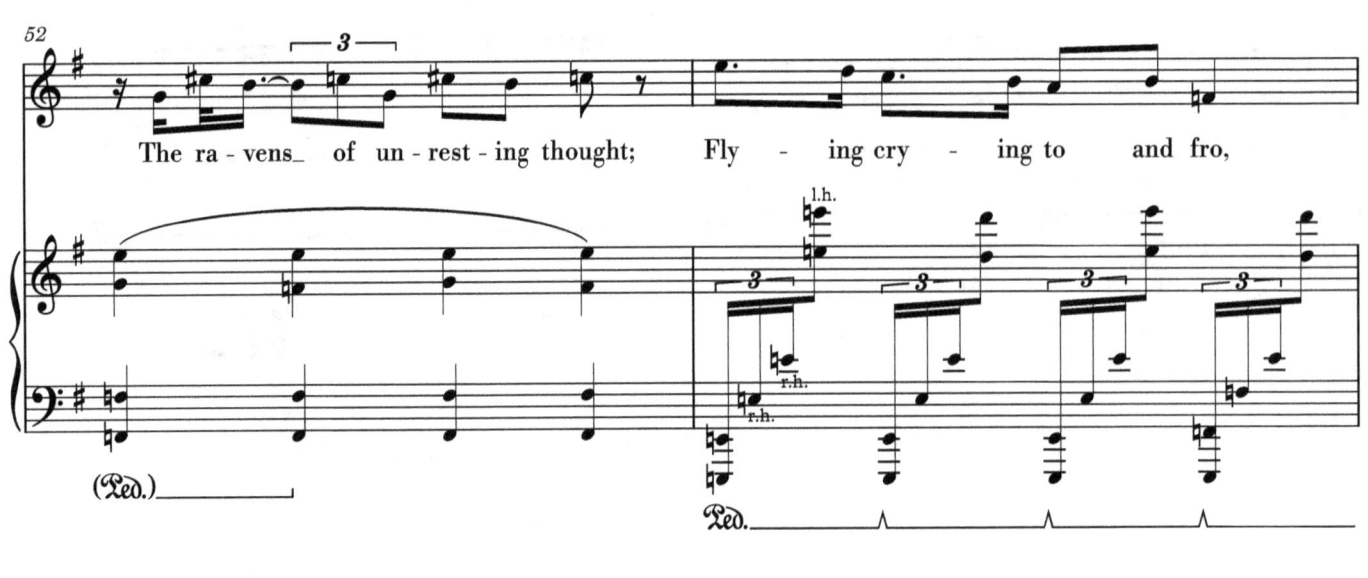
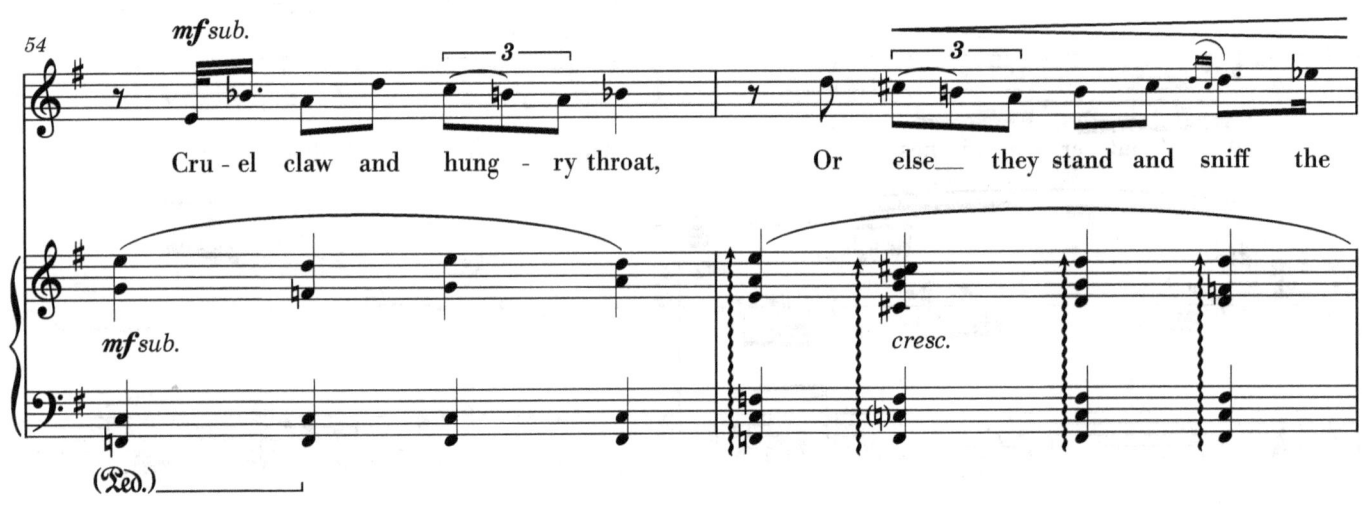

Commissioned by The Cincinnati Review

Mnemosyne

TODD HEARON
CARRIE MAGIN
(2016)

Copyright © 2016 by Two Places Publishing (ASCAP). All Rights Reserved.
Text from No Other Gods (Salmon Poetry, 2015). Copyright © 2015 by Tedd Hearon. Used with permission.

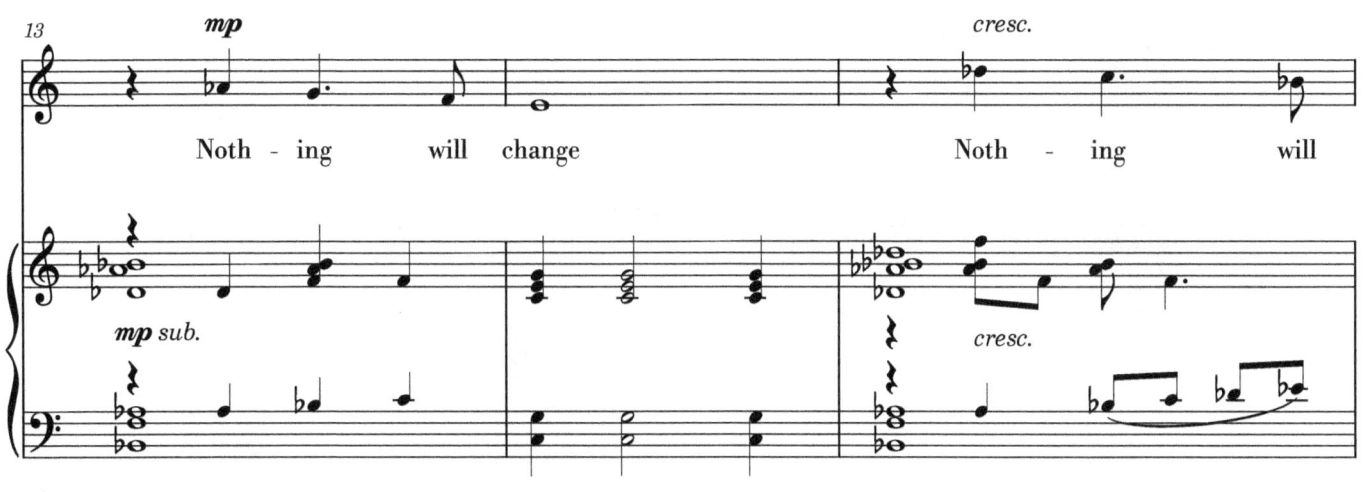
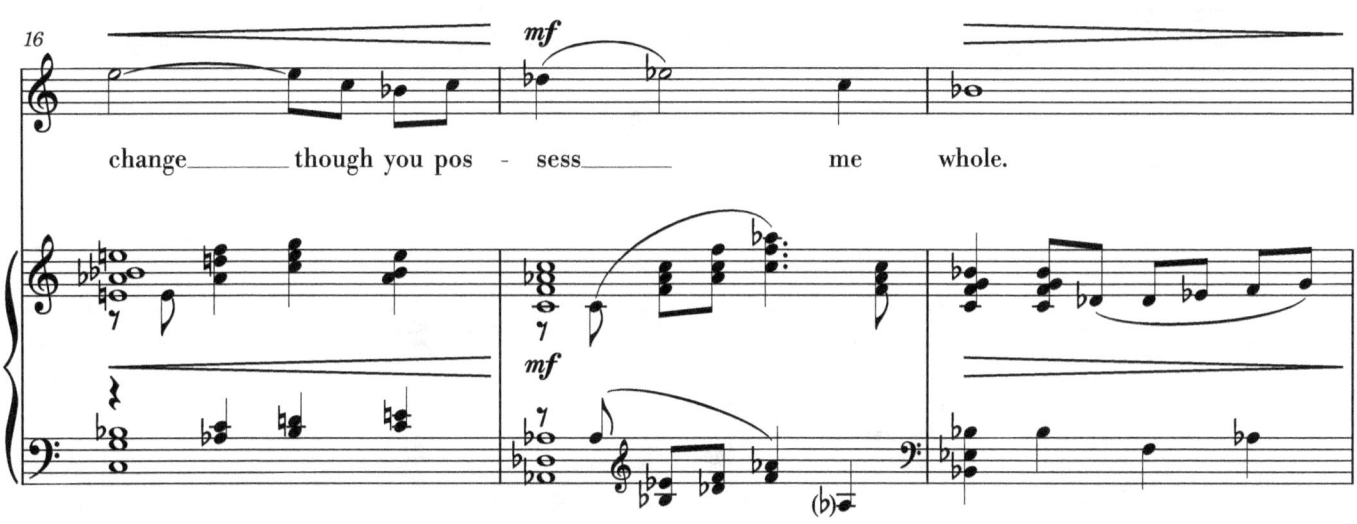

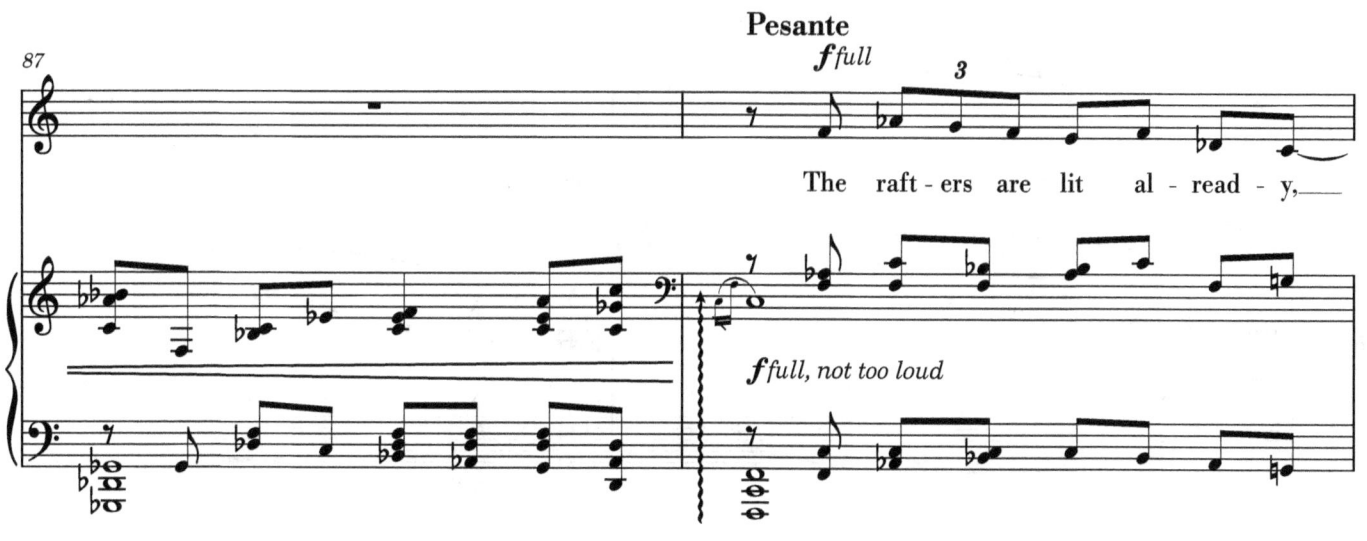

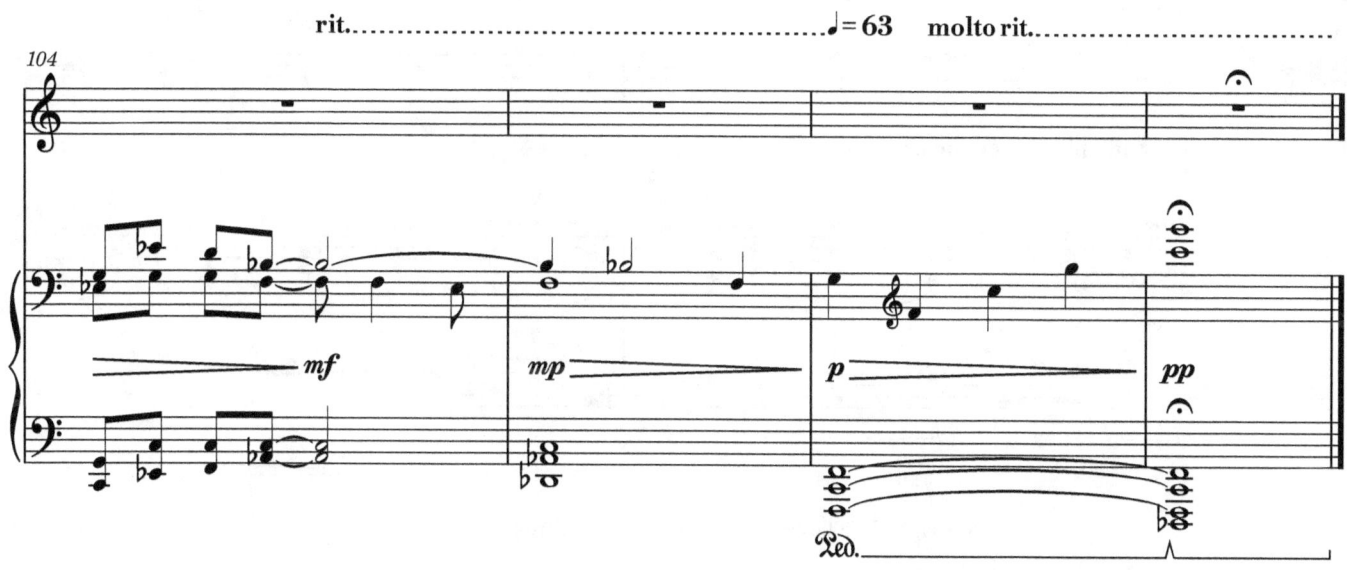

The Happiest Day, The Happiest Hour
from Edgar Allan Poe Song Cycle

EDGAR ALLAN POE

ALLEN MCCULLOUGH
(2004)

Copyright © 2004 by Allen McCullough. All Rights Reserved.

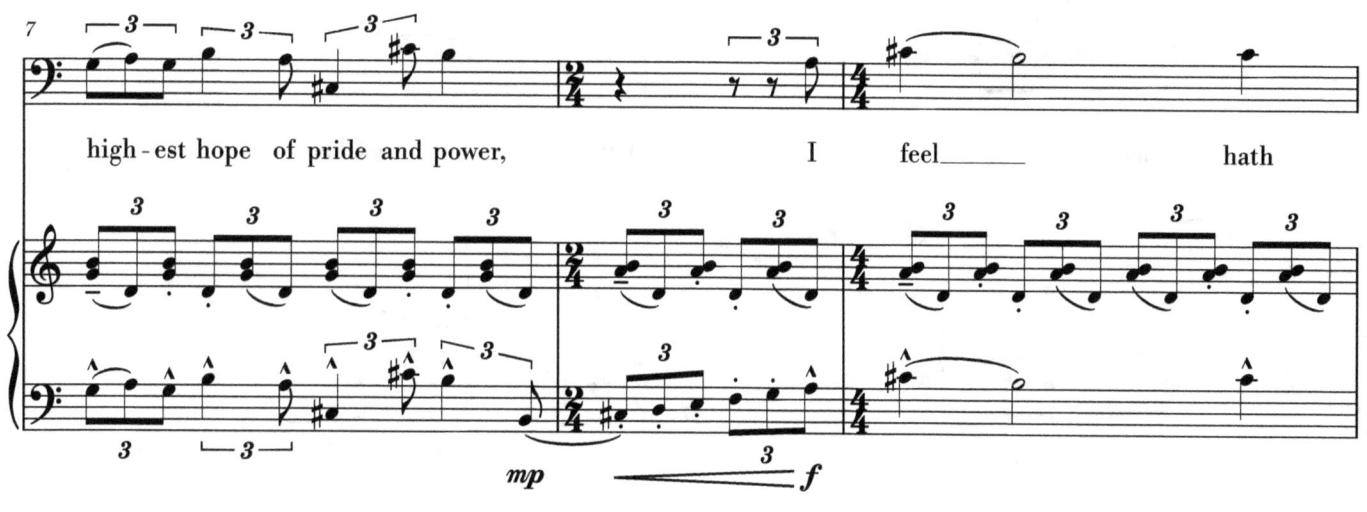
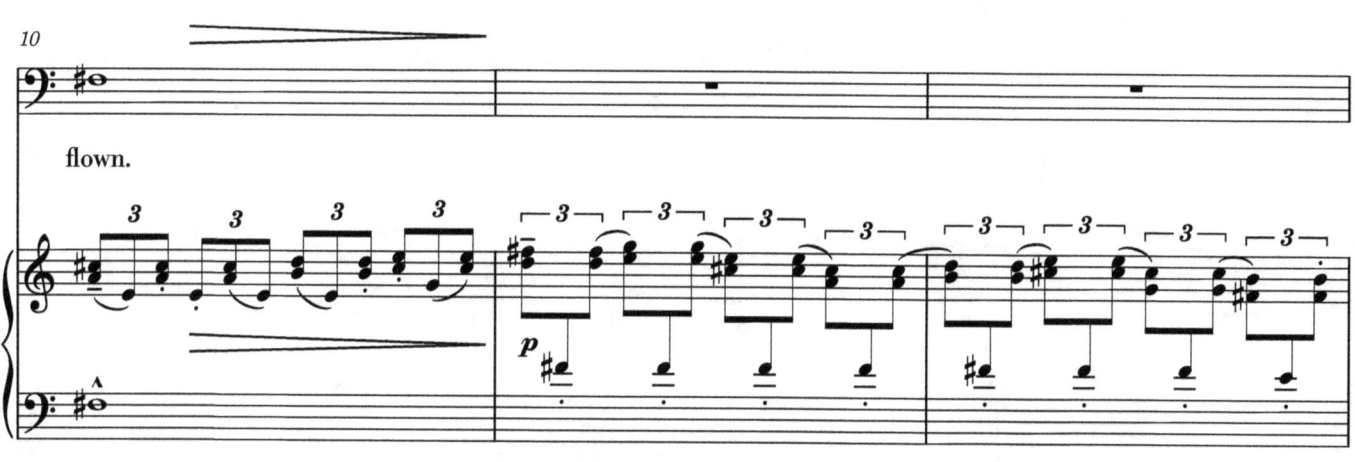

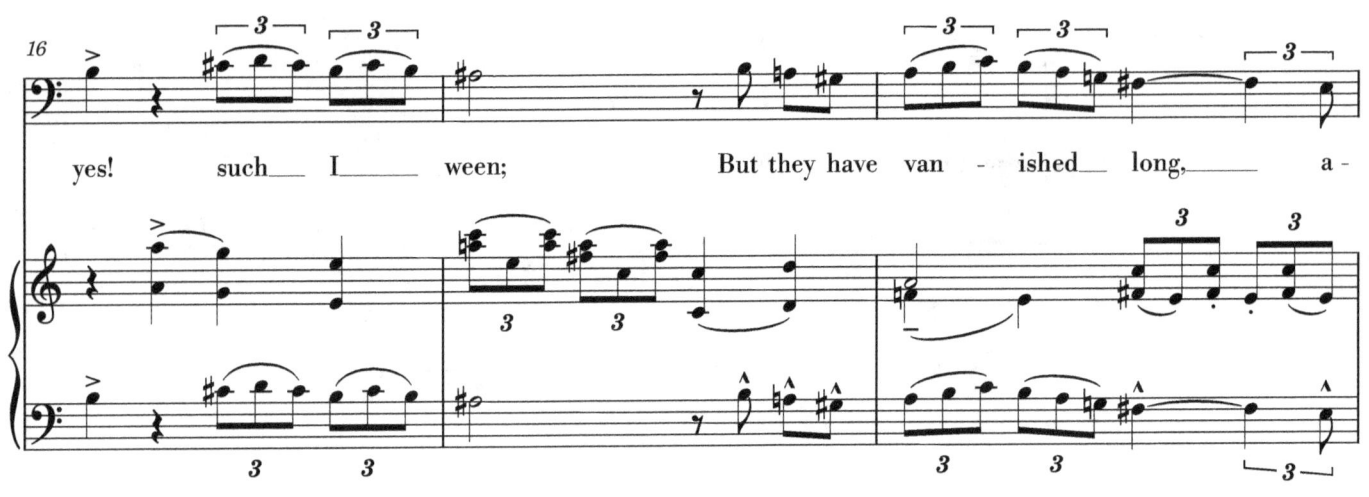

76

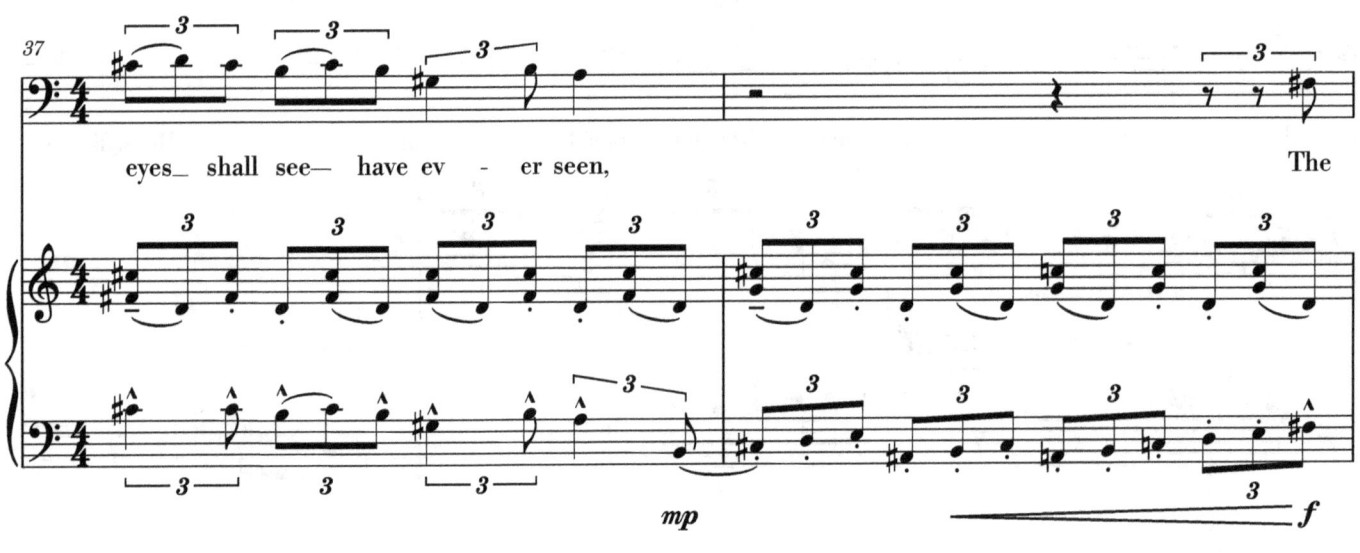

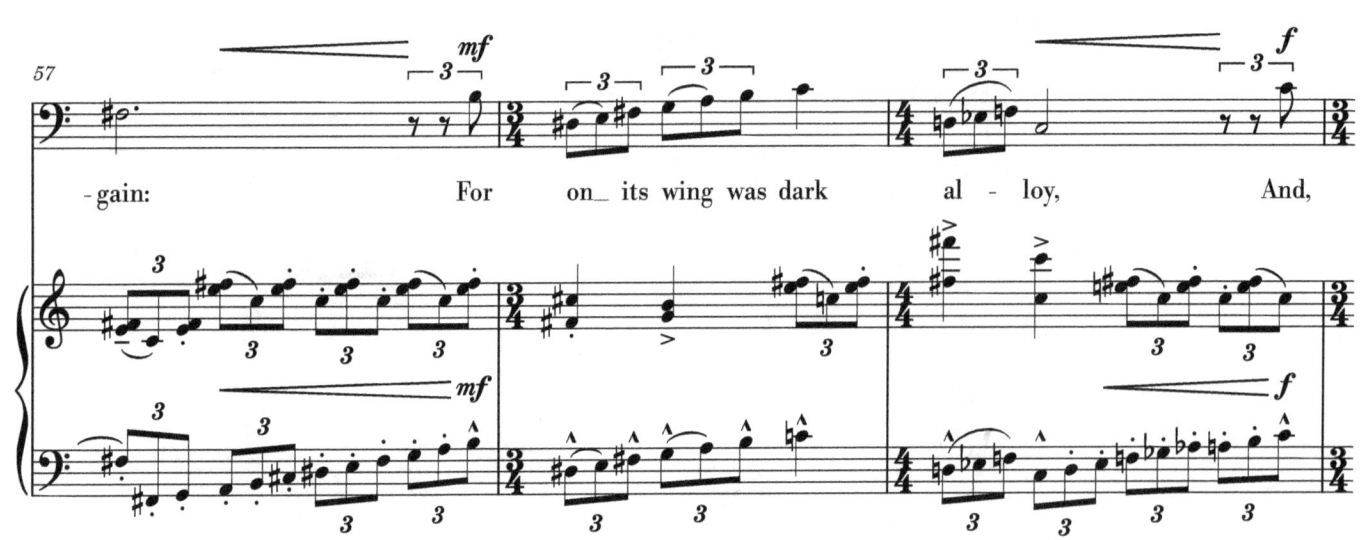

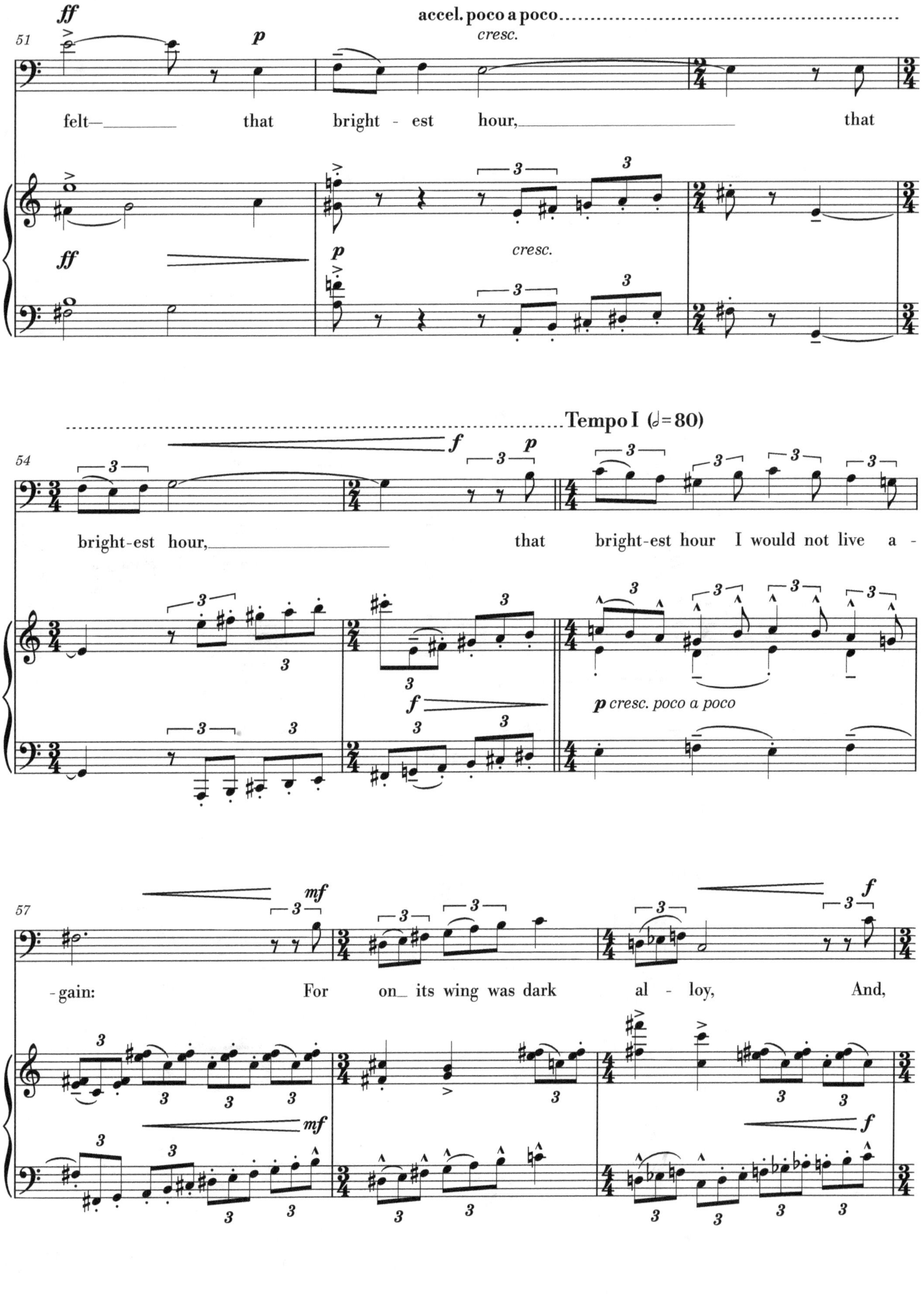
ff
accel. poco a poco
cresc.
51
p
felt— that bright - est hour, that
3
3
ff
p
cresc.
Tempo I (𝅗𝅥=80)
f
p
54
bright-est hour, that bright-est hour I would not live a -
f
p cresc. poco a poco
mf
57
-gain: For on its wing was dark al - loy, And,
mf
f

(Song of) Innisfail

THOMAS MOORE

RYAN MOLLOY
(2012)

Copyright © 2012 Ryan Molloy

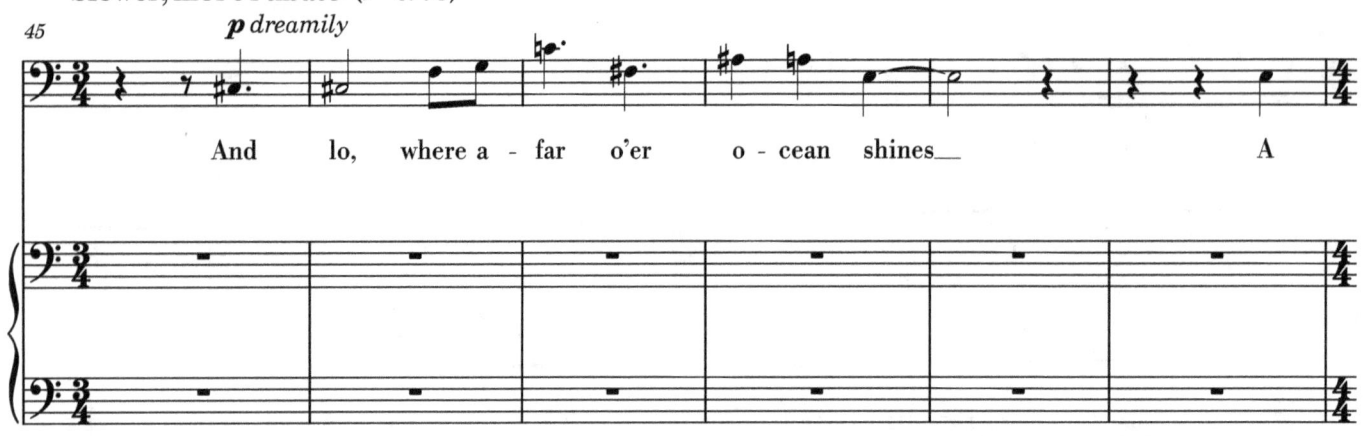

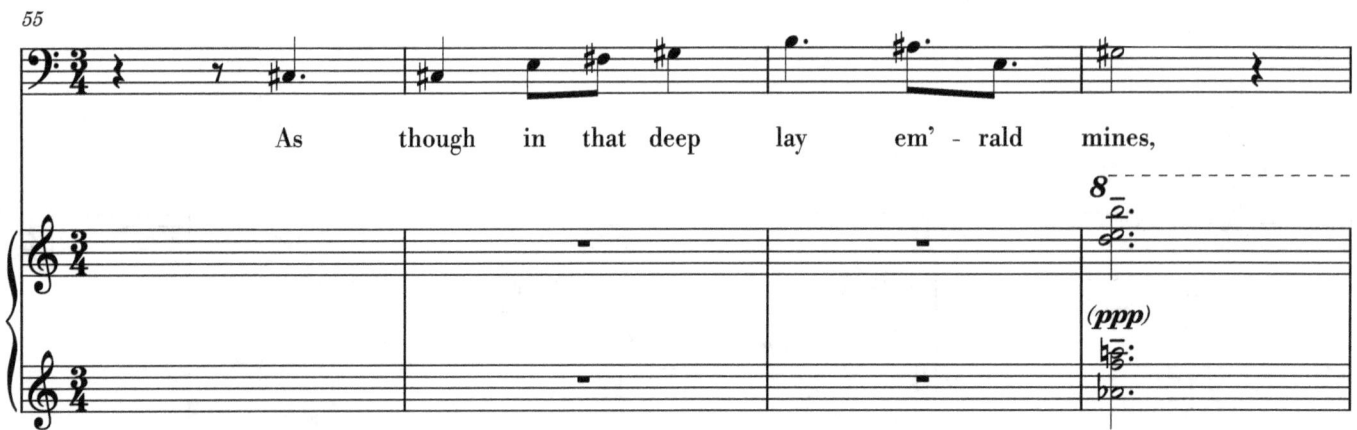

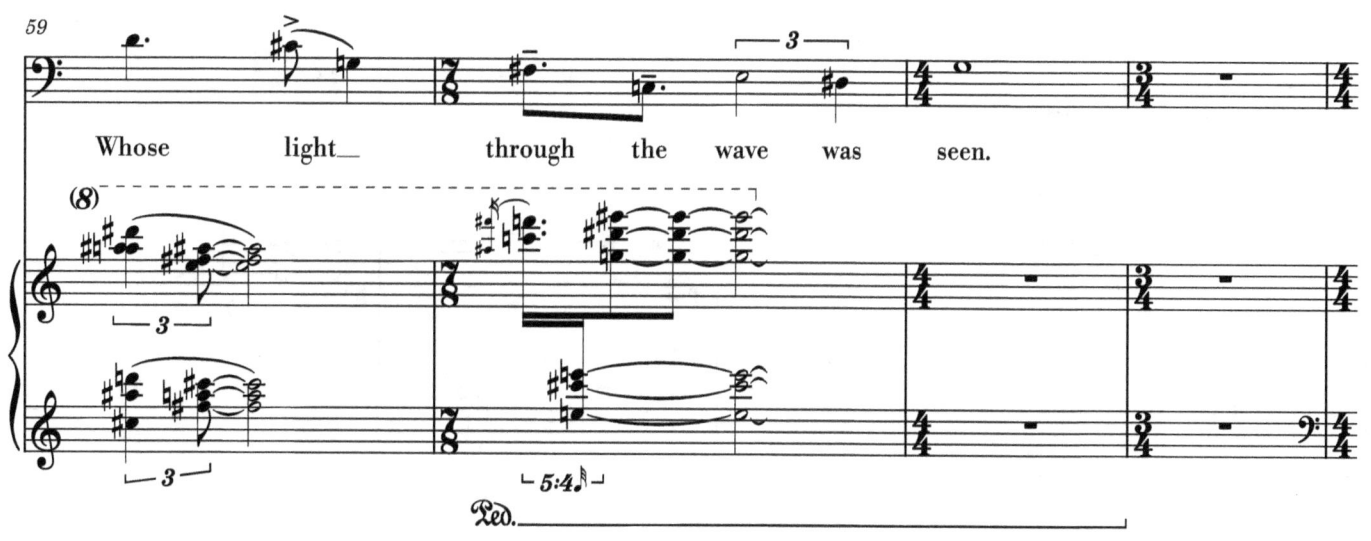

86

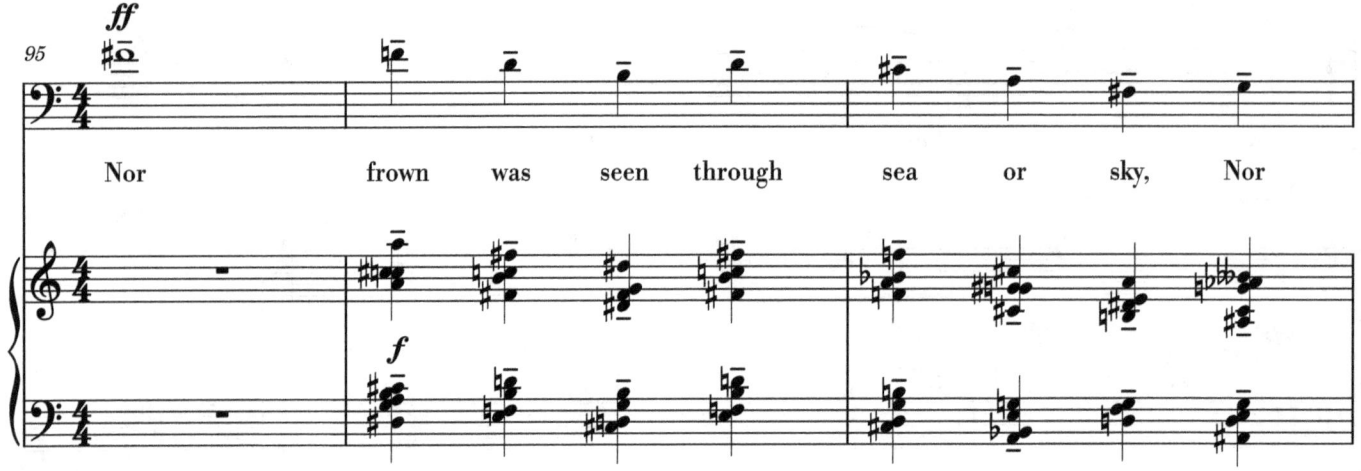

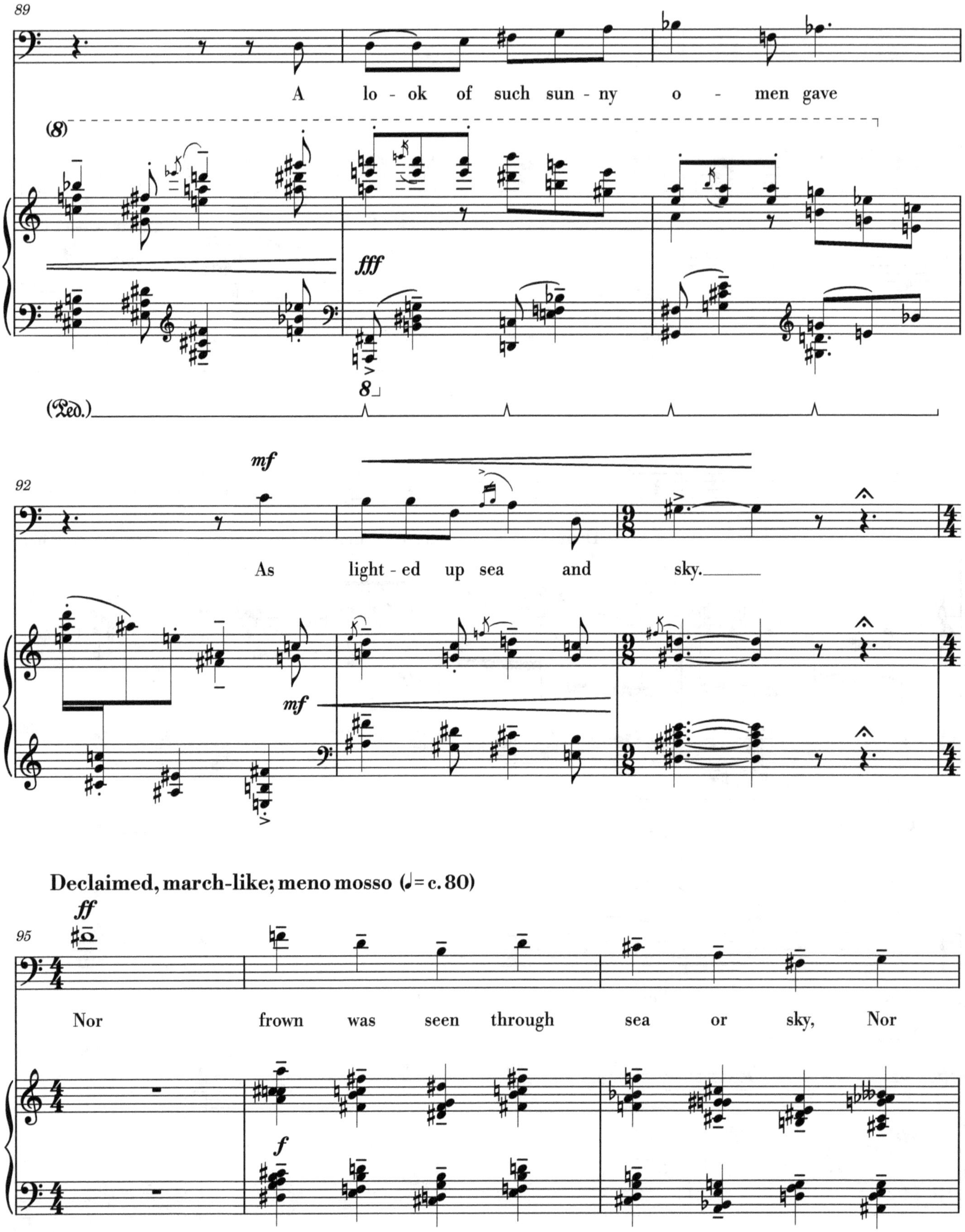
89
A lo - ok of such sun - ny o - men gave
(8)
fff
8
(Ped.)
92
mf
As light - ed up sea and sky.
mf
Declaimed, march-like; meno mosso (♩= c. 80)
ff
95
Nor frown was seen through sea or sky, Nor
f

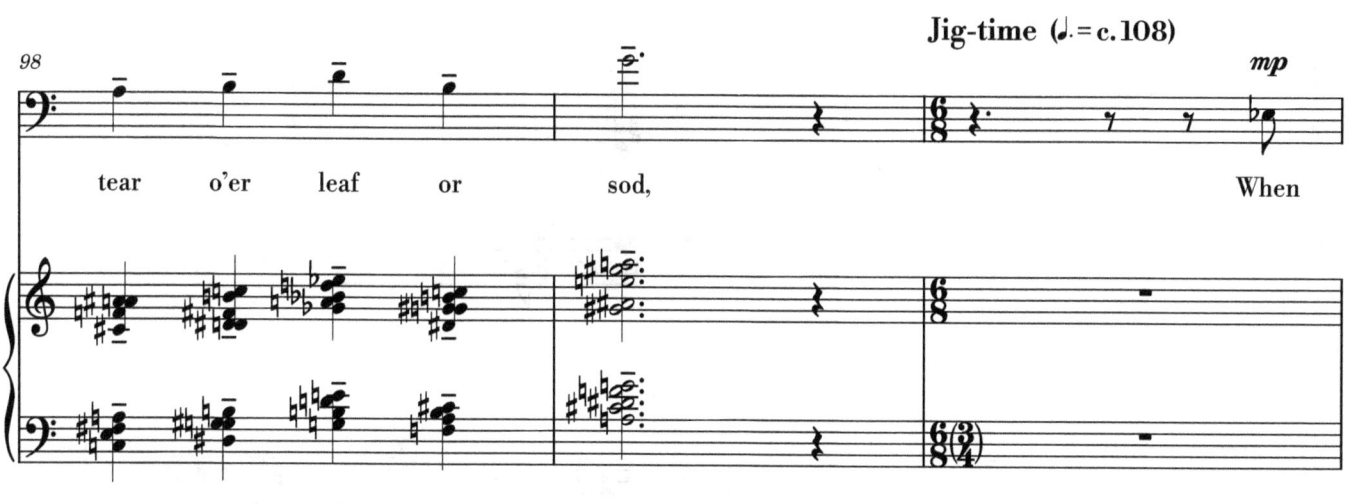

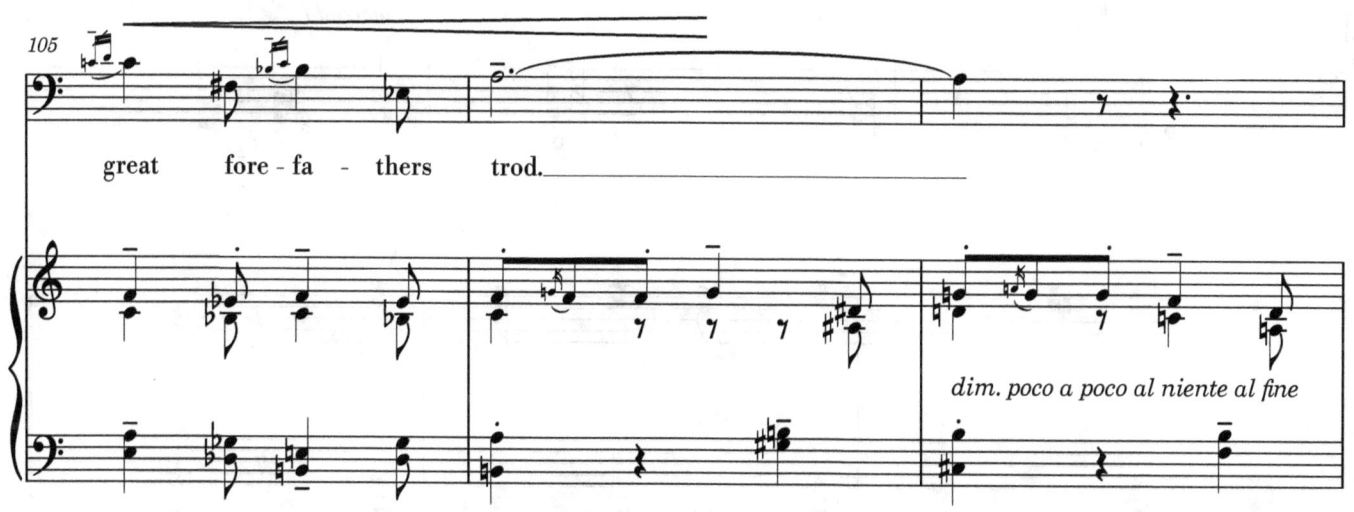

Belfast
27.iv.2012

Love Remained
from the song cycle Love Remained

MICHAEL KELLY*

BEN MOORE
(2011)

* The poem is based on a memory of a family vacation:
two brothers running on the beach near Diamond Head in Hawaii.

Copyright © 2011 by Ben Moore. All Rights Reserved.
Text copyright © 2011 by Michael Kelly. Used by permission.

94

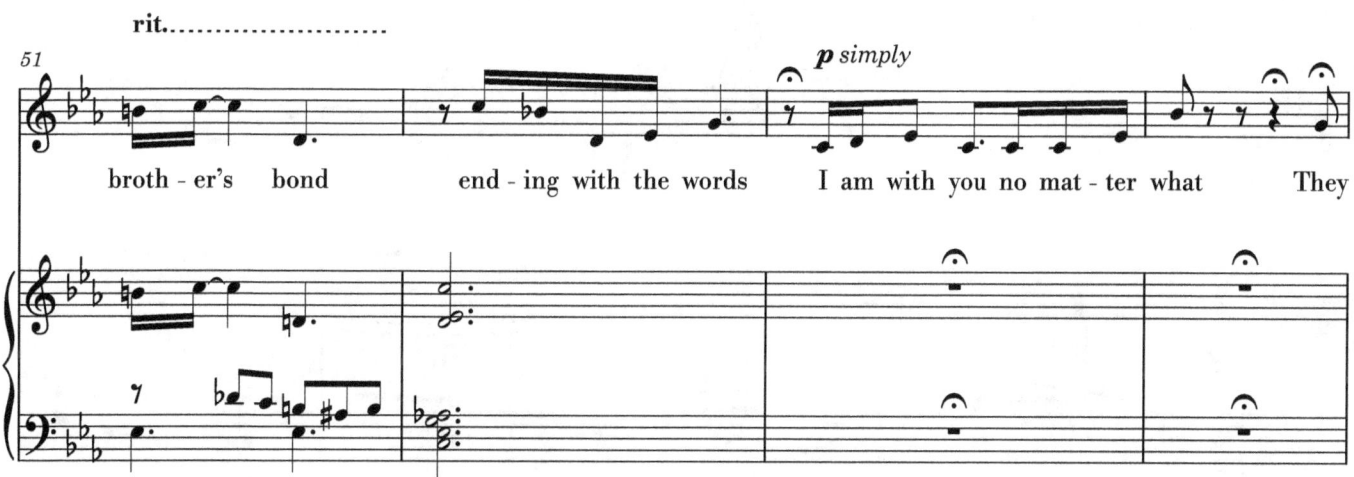

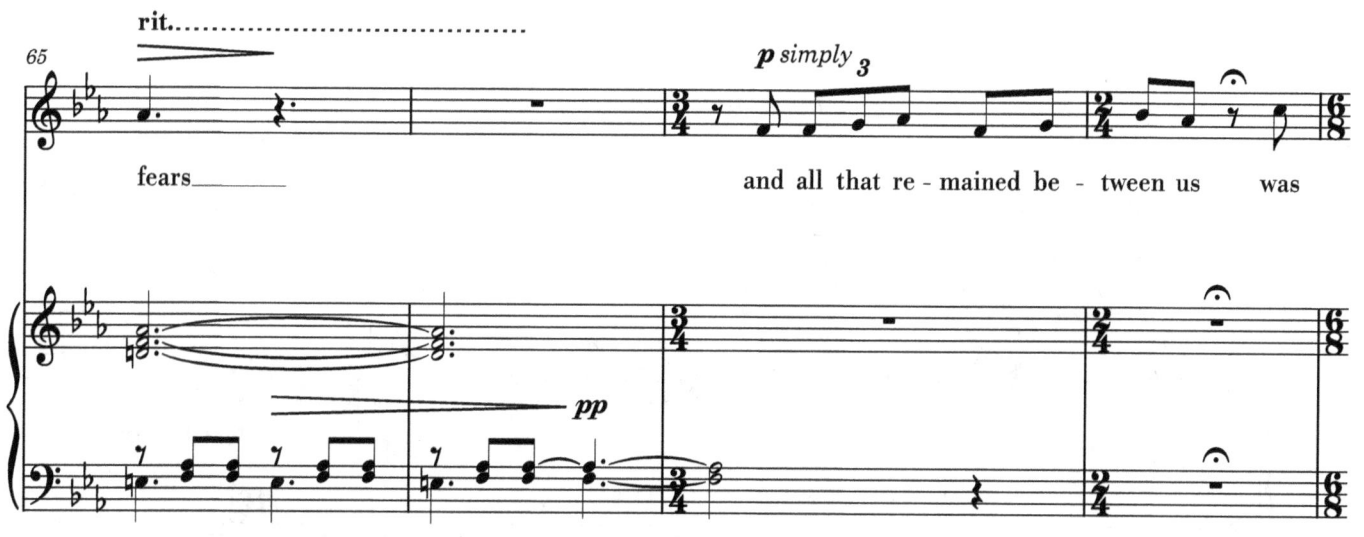
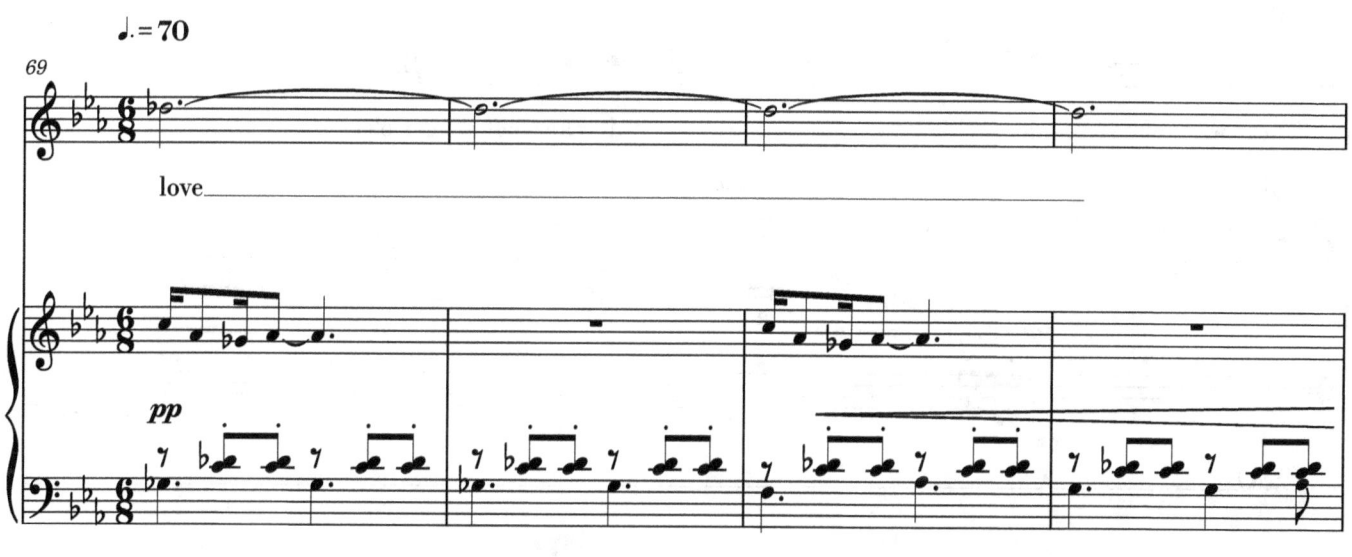

The Water is Wide
from Three Folk Songs

TRADITIONAL GABRIELLE ROSSE OWENS
(2016)

* Accidentals hold throughout the system

Copyright © 2016 by Gabrielle Owens (ASCAP)

100

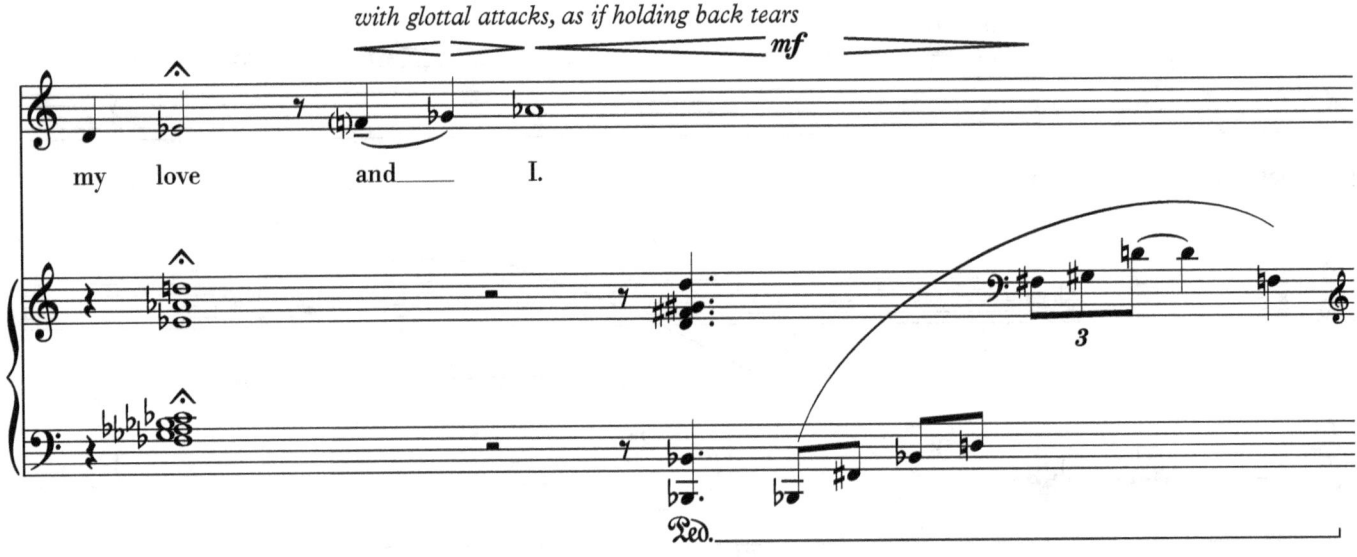
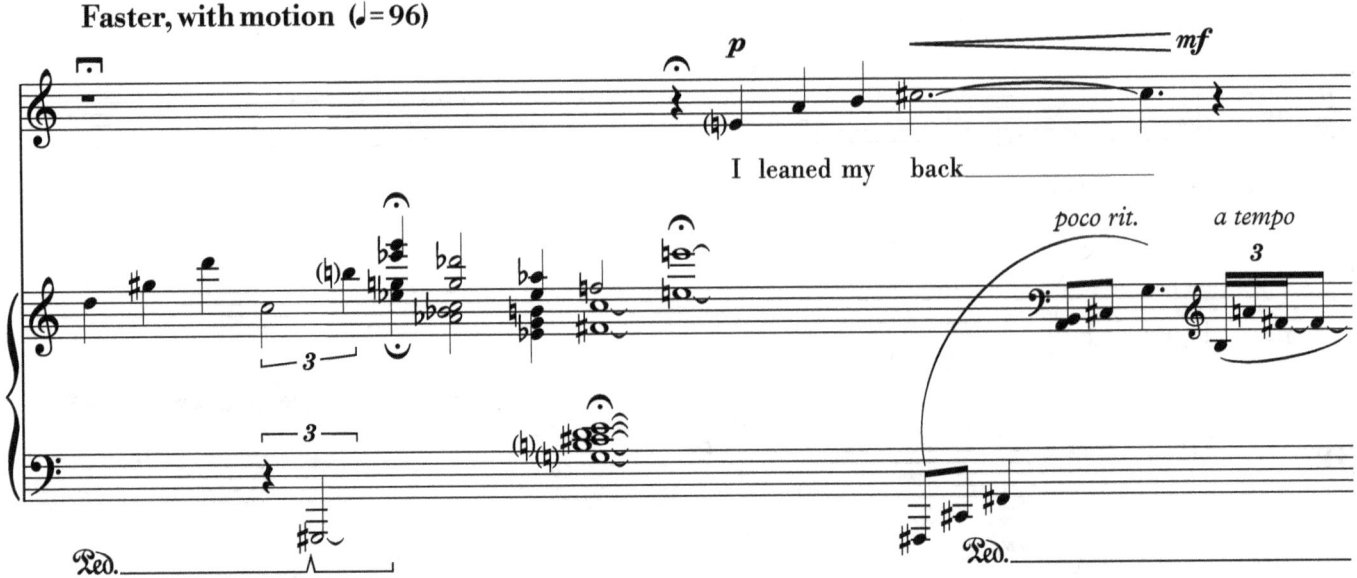

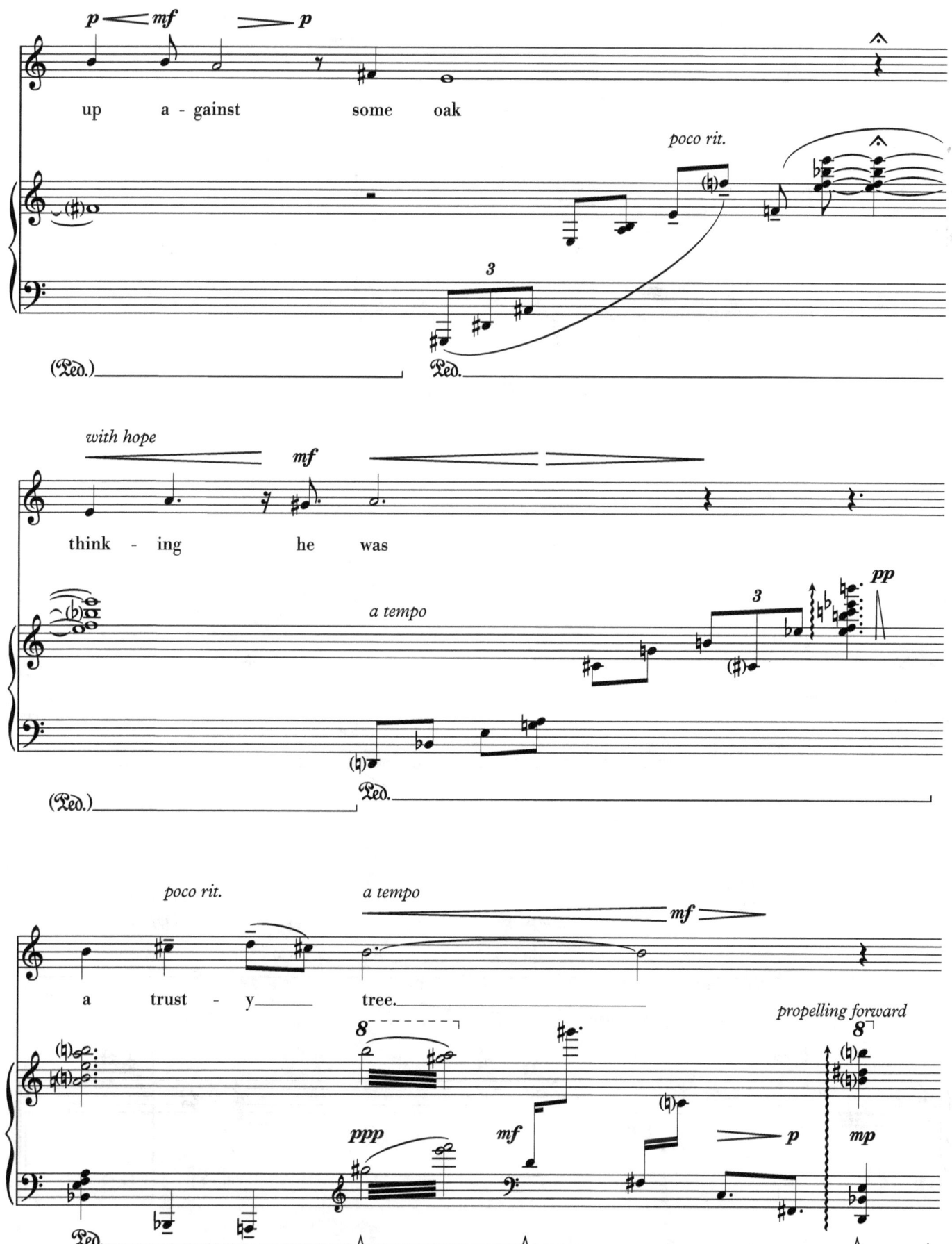

Alley Cat Love Song
from Bad Pets

Dana Gioia

Paul Salerni
(2007)

Copyright © 2007 by Paul Salerni. All Right Reserved.
Text copyright © 2007 by Dana Gioia. Used with permission.

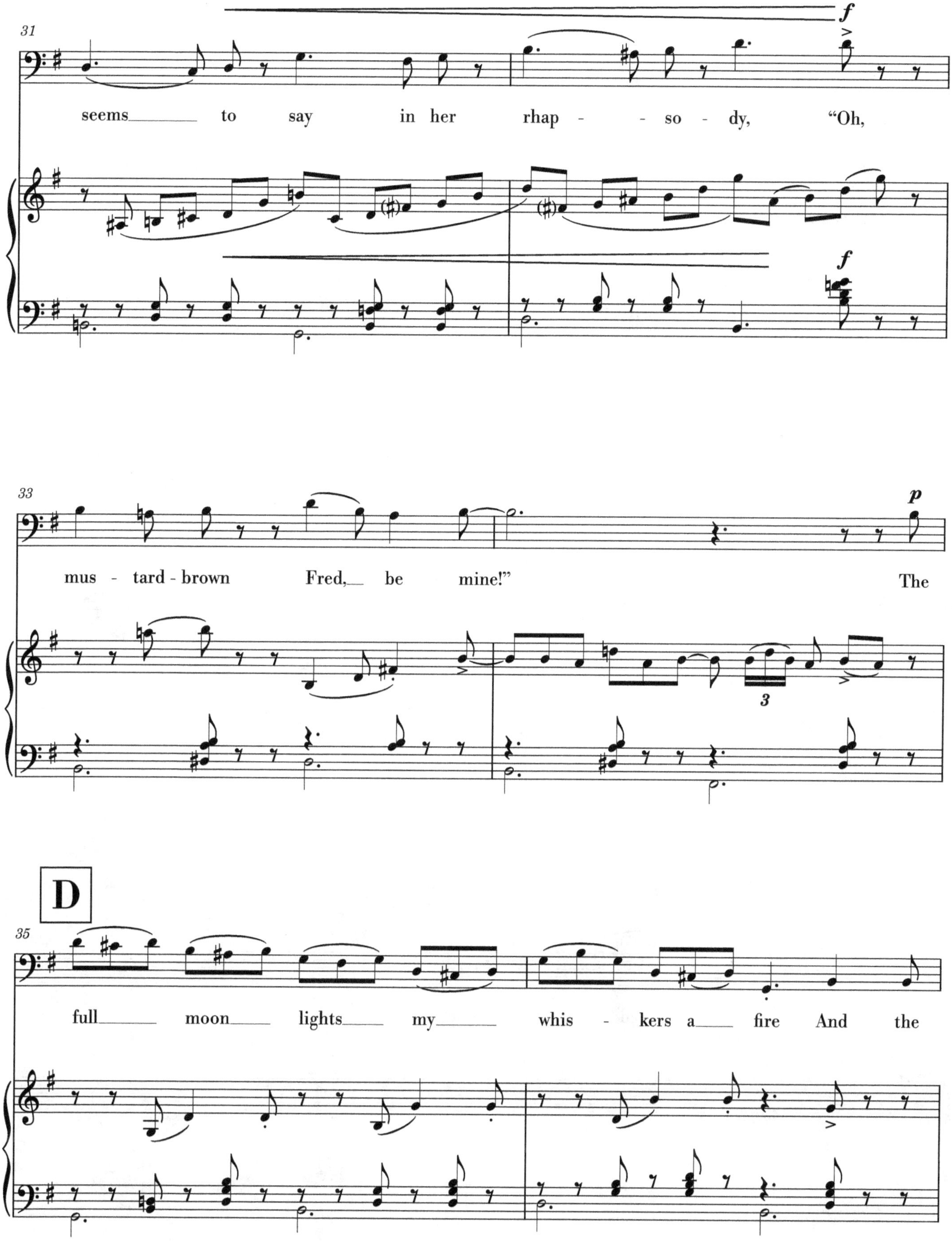
31
f
seems___ to say in her rhap - - so - dy, "Oh,
f
33
p
mus - tard - brown Fred,_ be mine!" The
3
D
35
full___ moon___ lights___ my___ whis - kers a___ fire And the

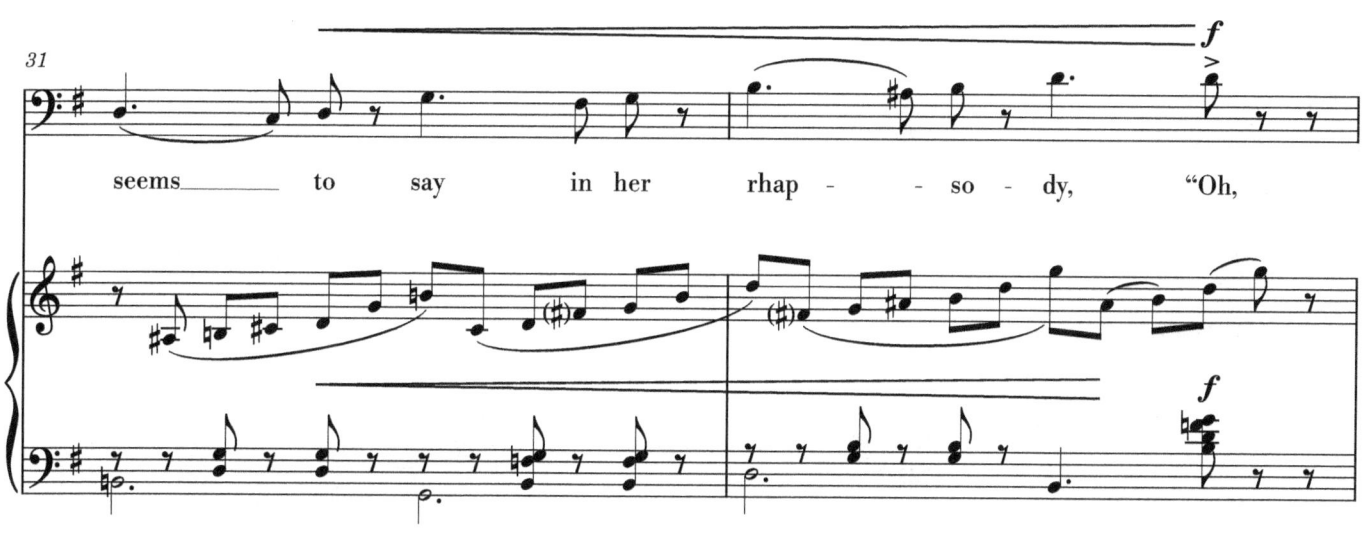

This Living Hand
from The Keats Cycle

JOHN KEATS HARRY STAFYLAKIS
(2007)

Mournful (♩=50) *poco rall.*

mp rubato

Lyrics: This liv-ing hand, this liv-ing hand, this liv-ing hand...

pp sotto voce

mf dolce

Copyright © 2007 Haralabos Stafylakis (ASCAP for the USA, SOCAN for the World) and Staves Obsidian Publishing (ASCAP), all rights reserved.

Commissioned by the Hourglass Ensemble, Sydney, Australia

There is a Solemn Wind Tonight

from Voices of a Northern Year

Katherine Mansfield

Margaret Tesch-Muller
(2016)

Copyright © by 2016 Margaret Tesch-Muller.

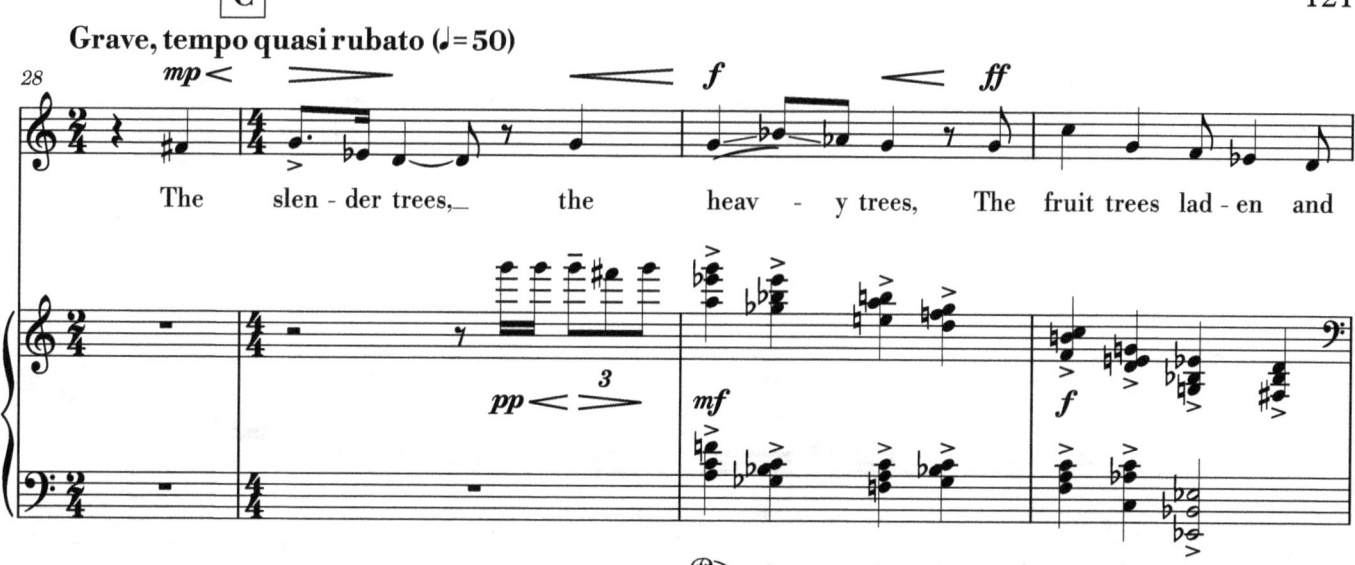

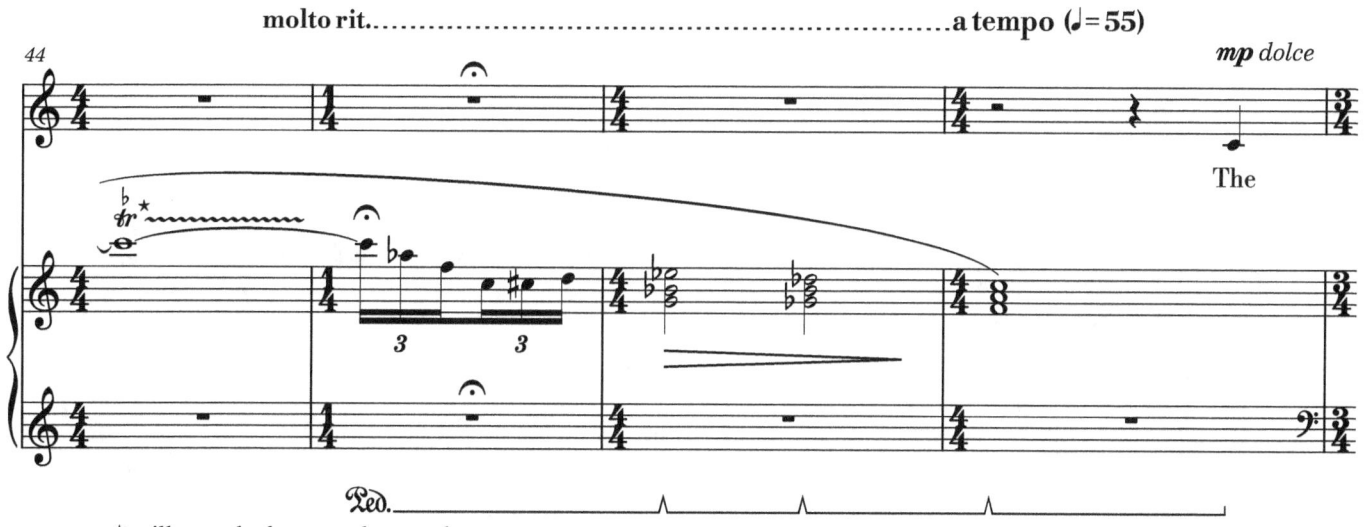

* trill speed: slow-moderate-slow

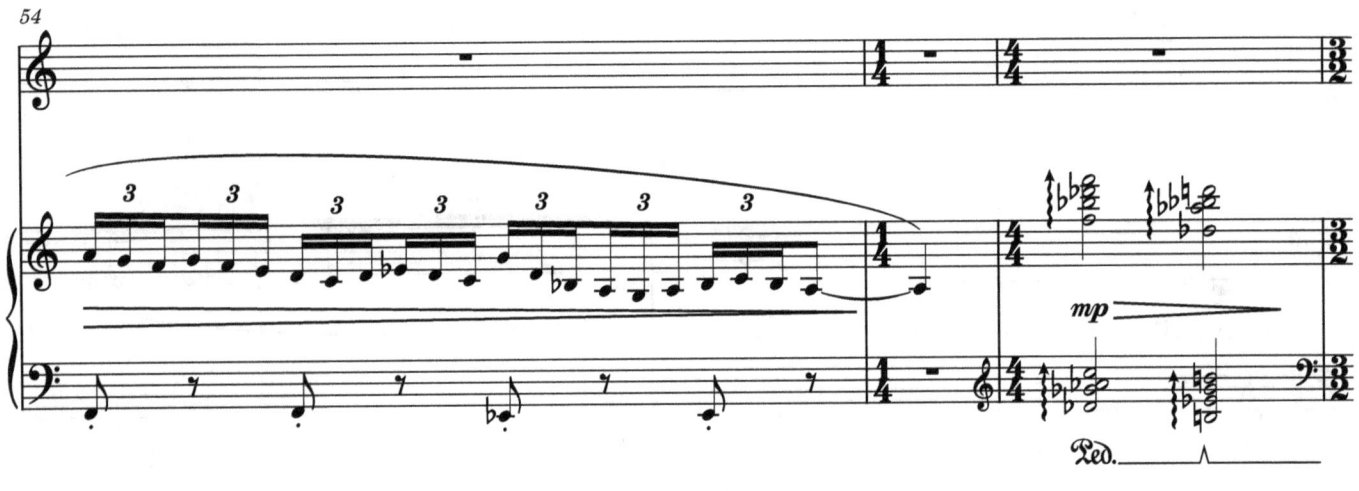

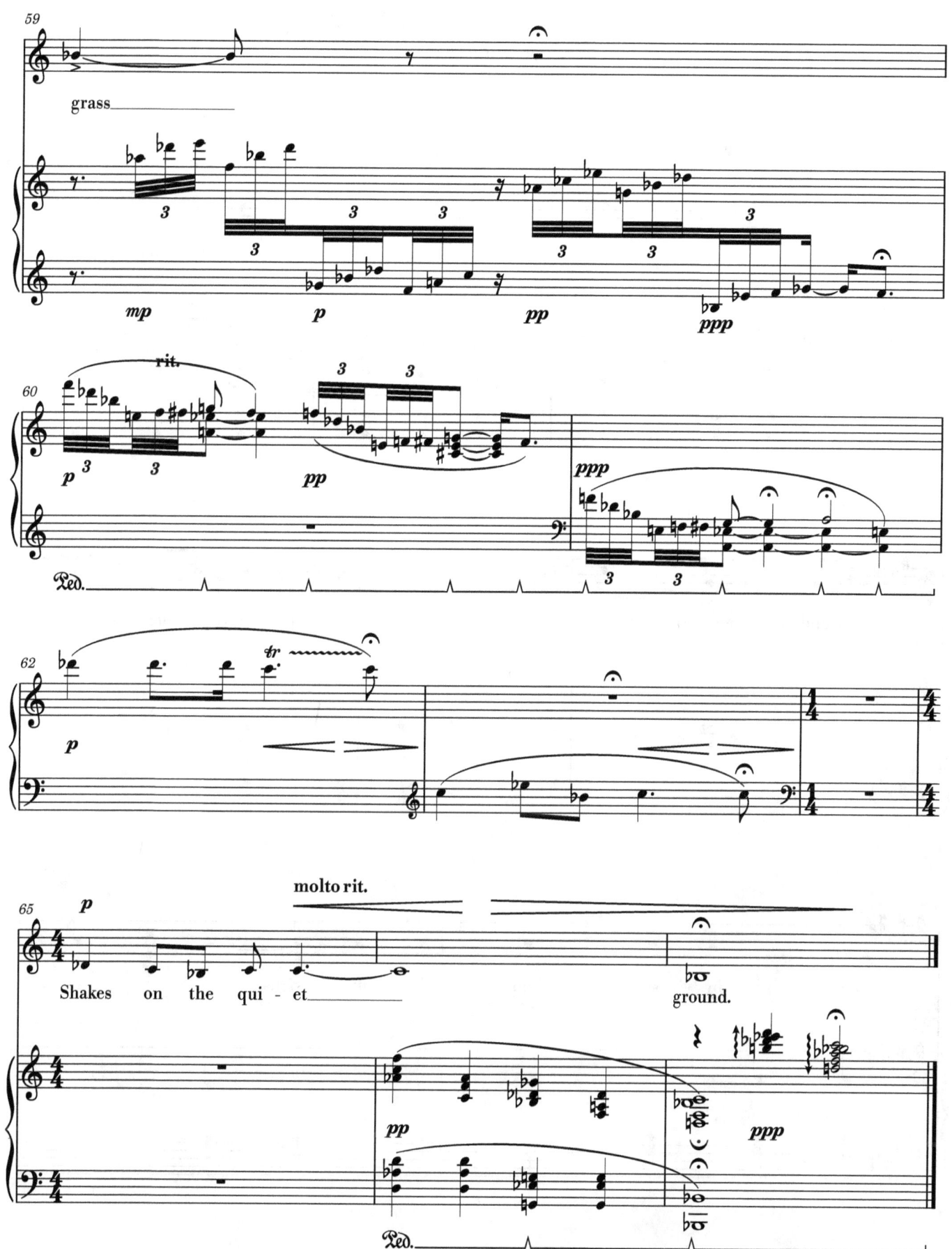

Among The Multitude
from Leaves

WALT WHITMAN

CRAIG URQUHART
(1980)

Copyright © 1980 by Craig Urquhart

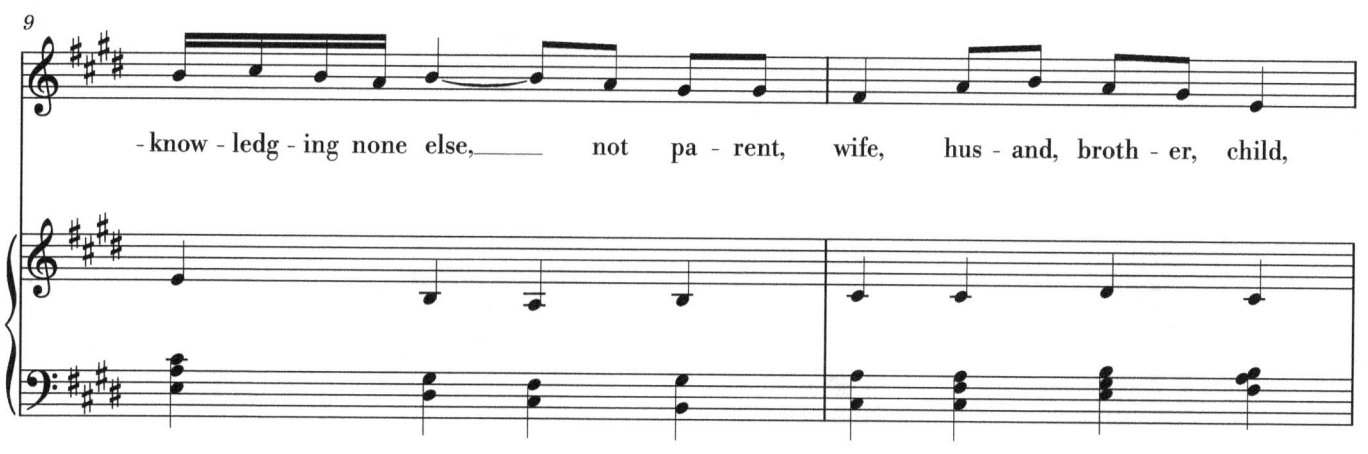

Looking Back at Spring

CONRAD WEISER

MARK LANZ WEISER
(2001)

Copyright © 2001 alltheweiser music (ASCAP).

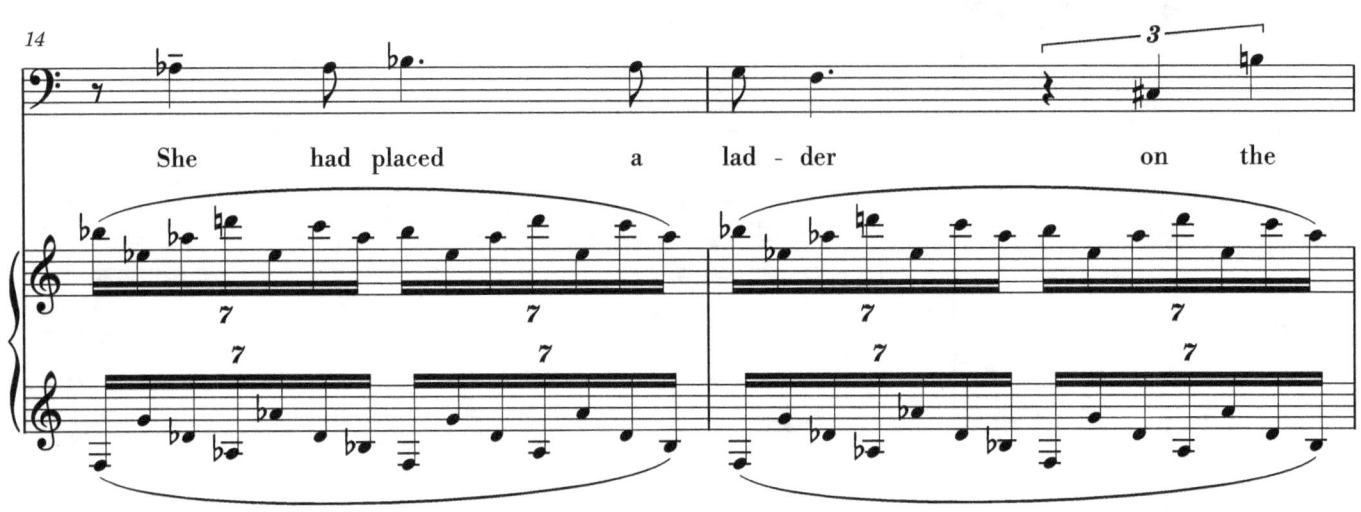

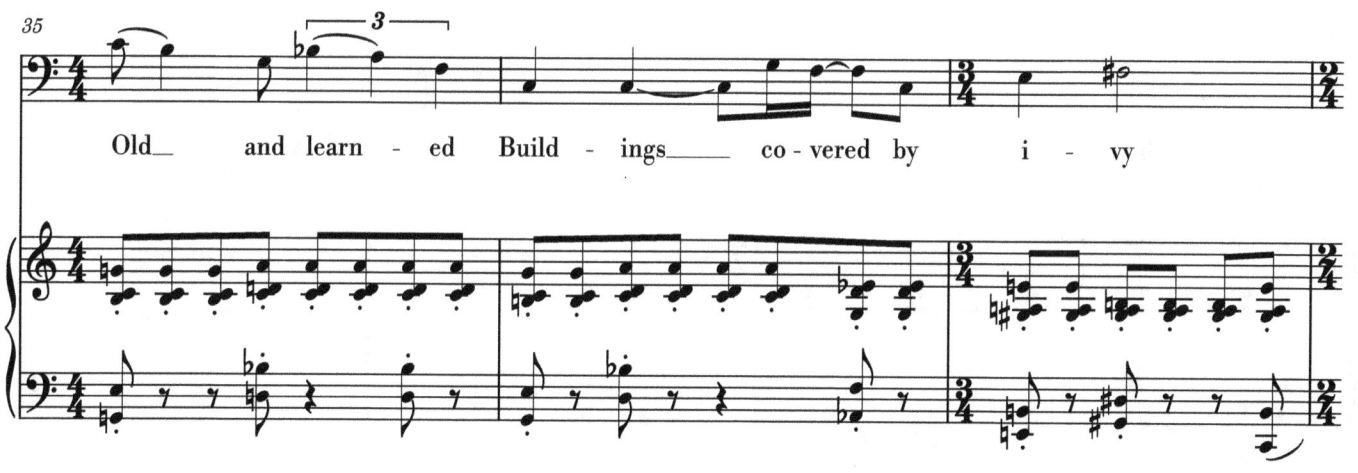

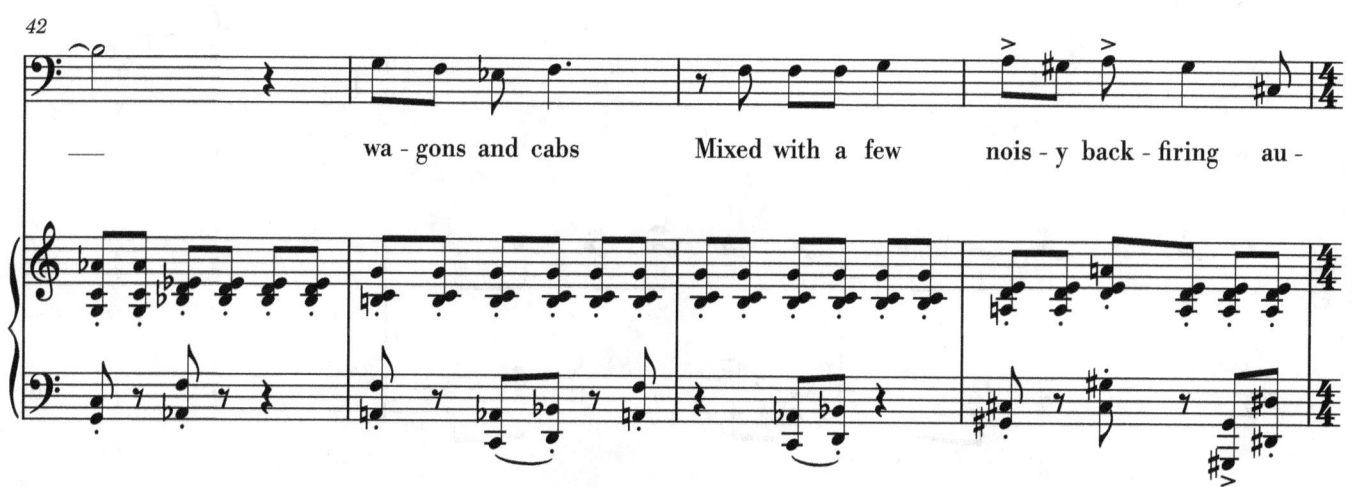

134

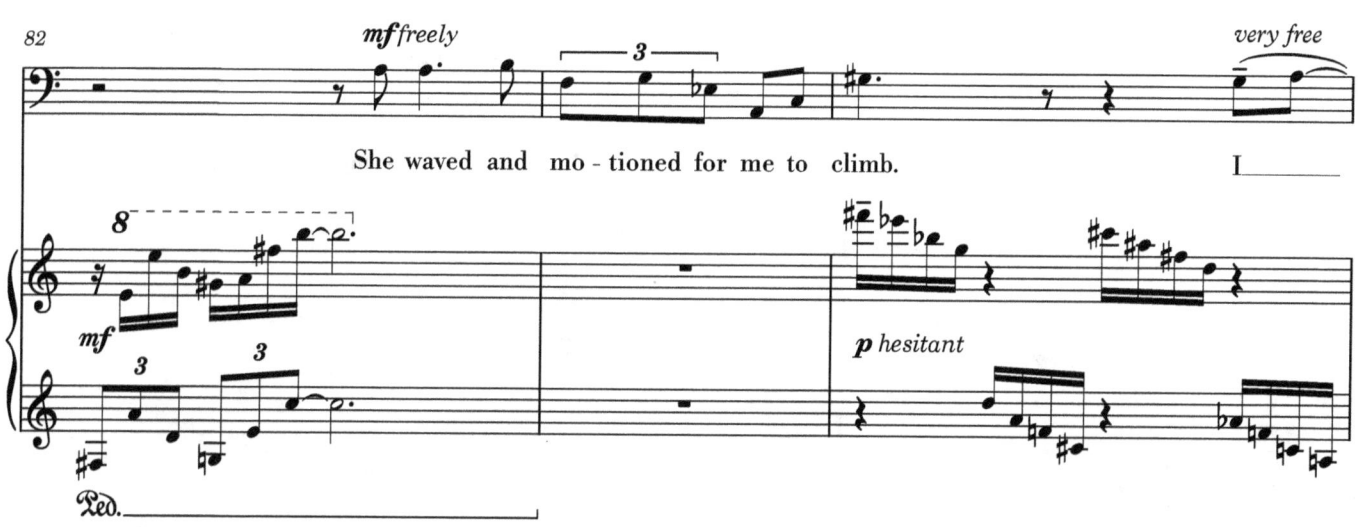

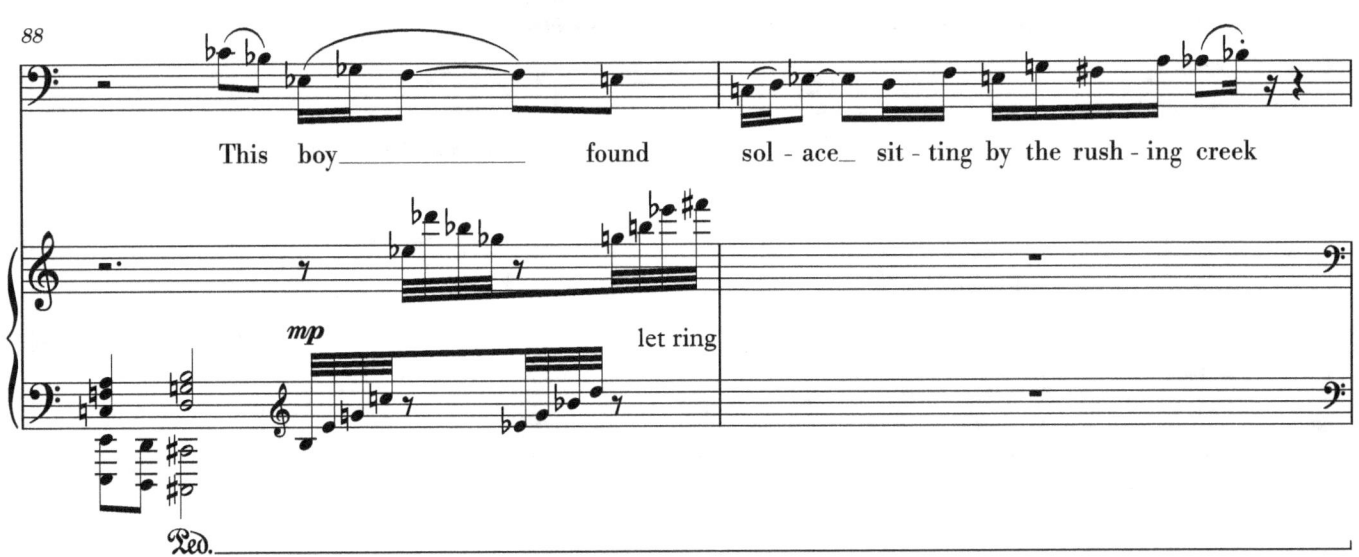

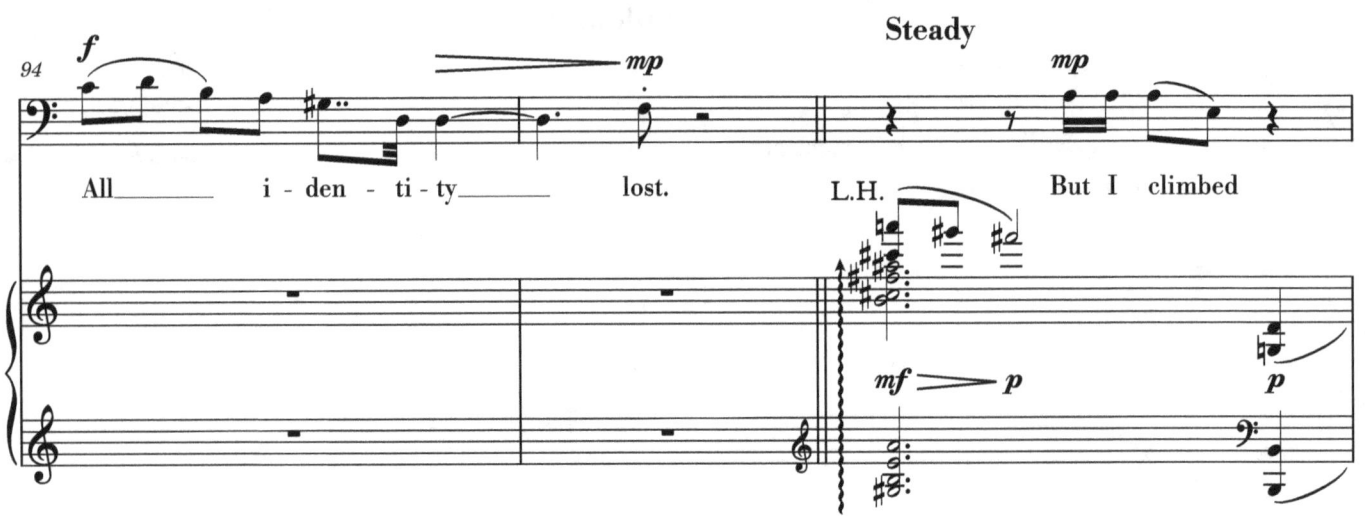

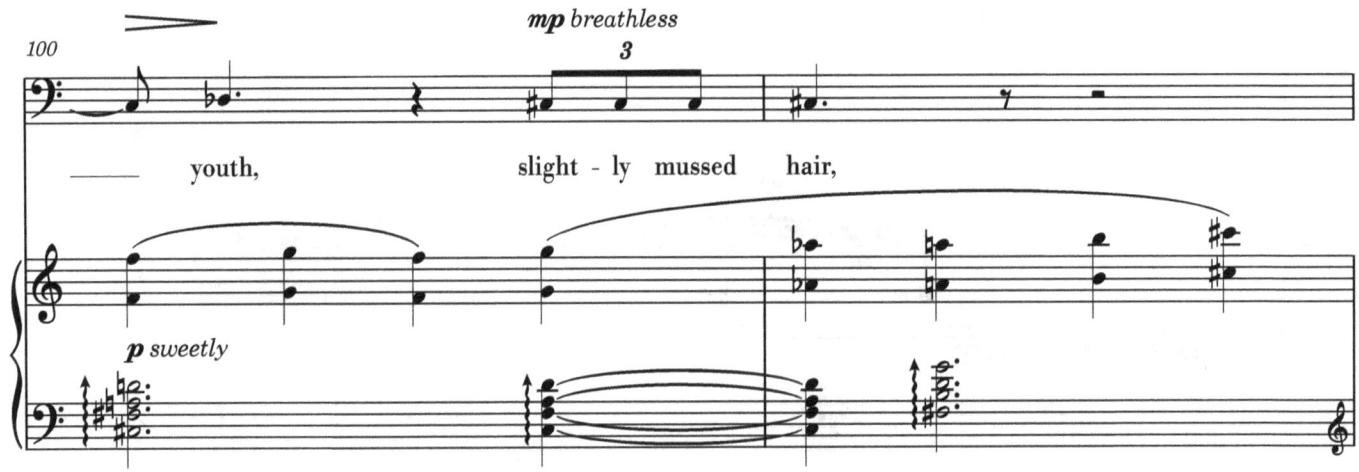

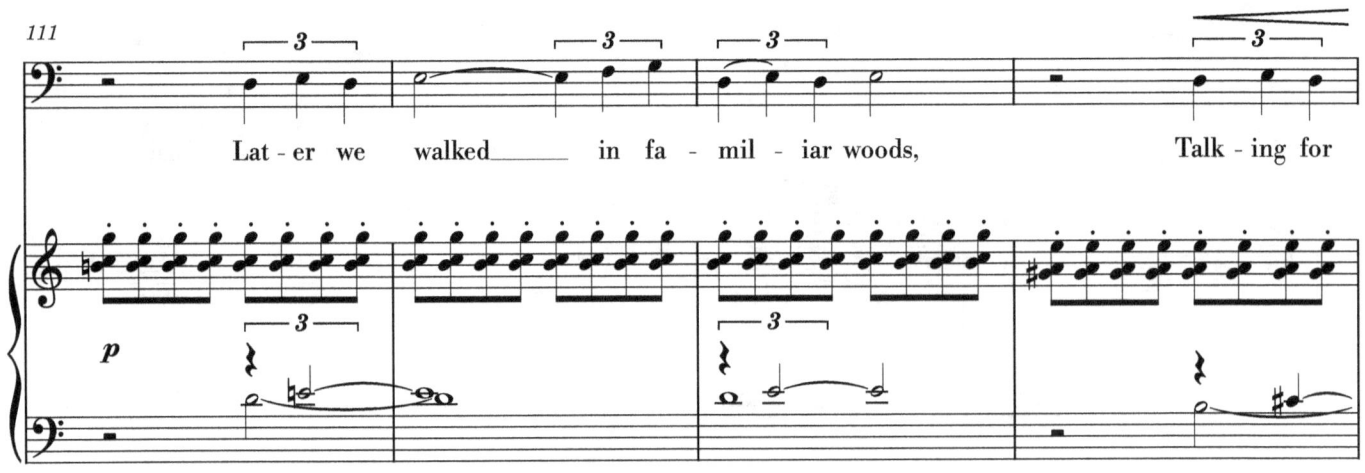

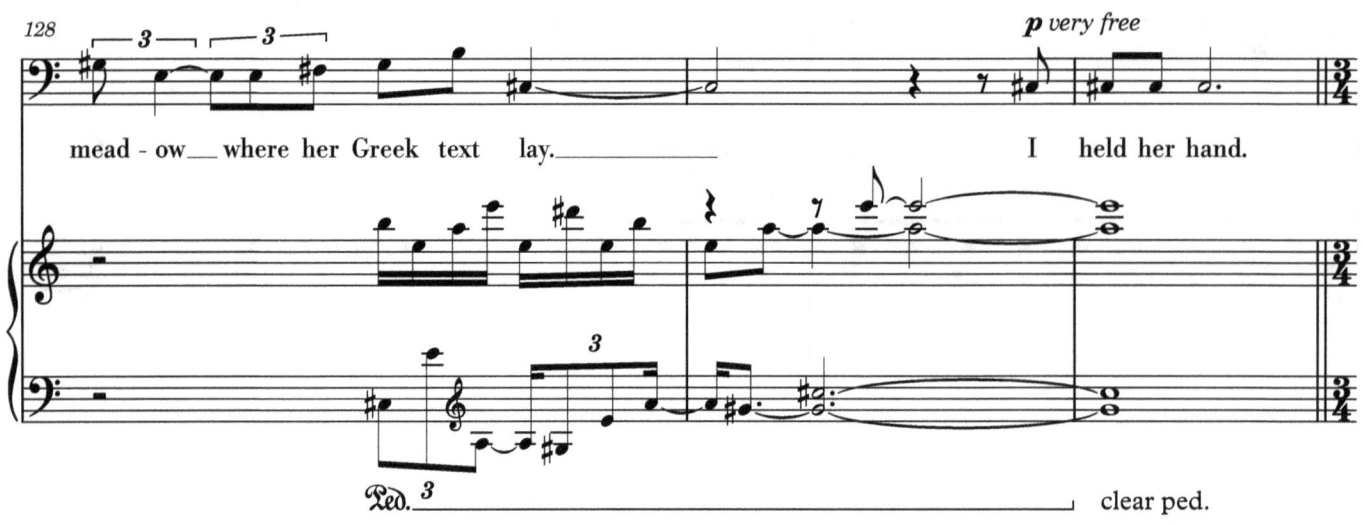
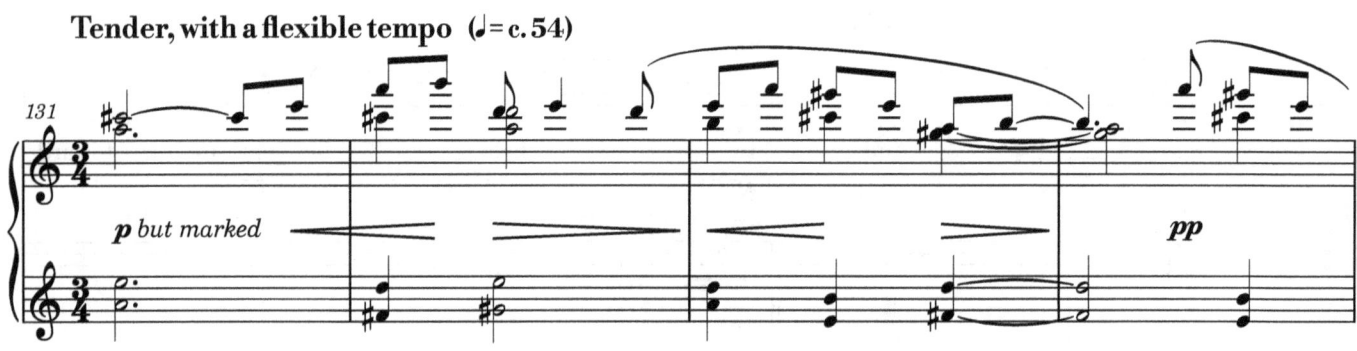

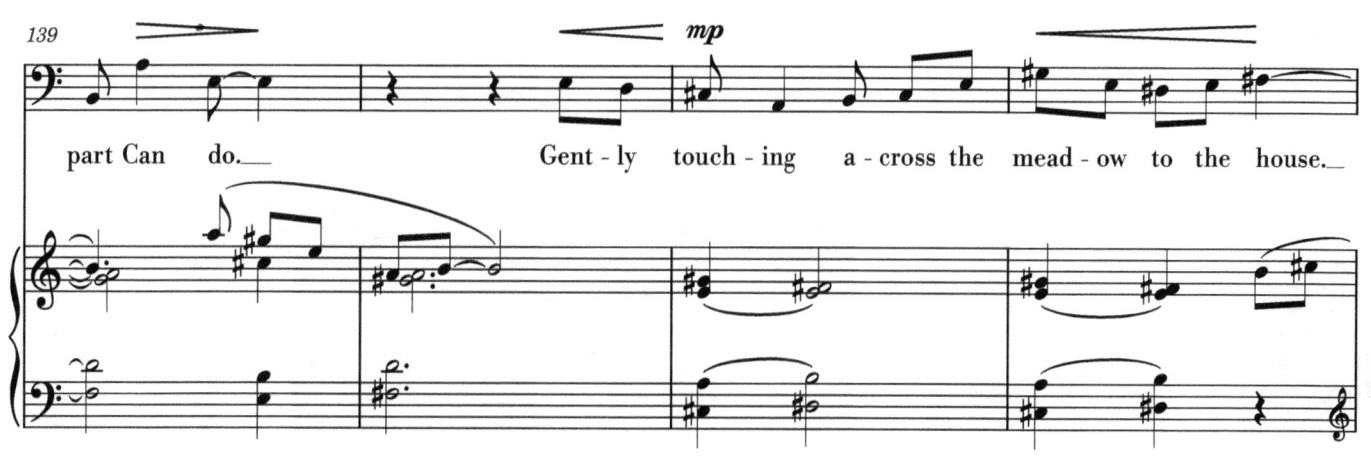
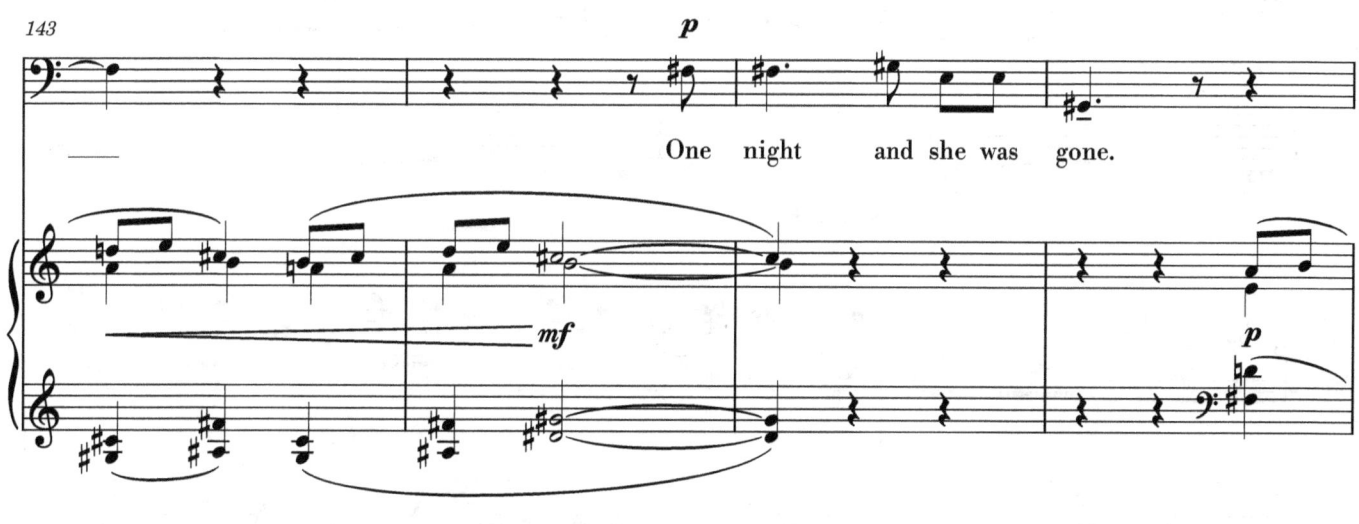

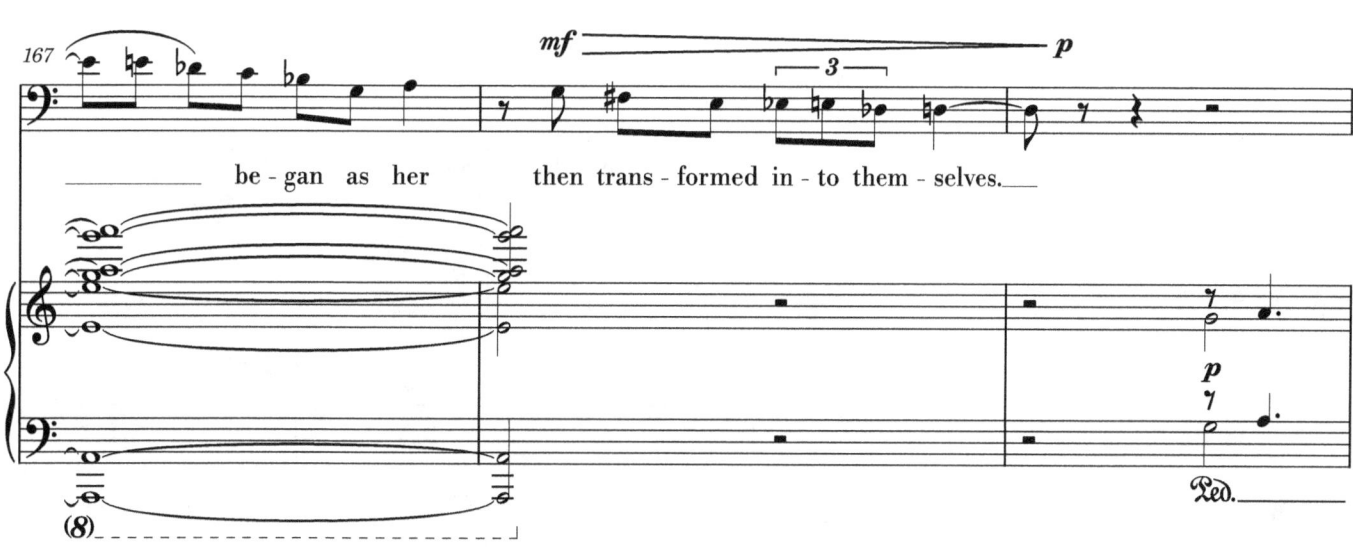

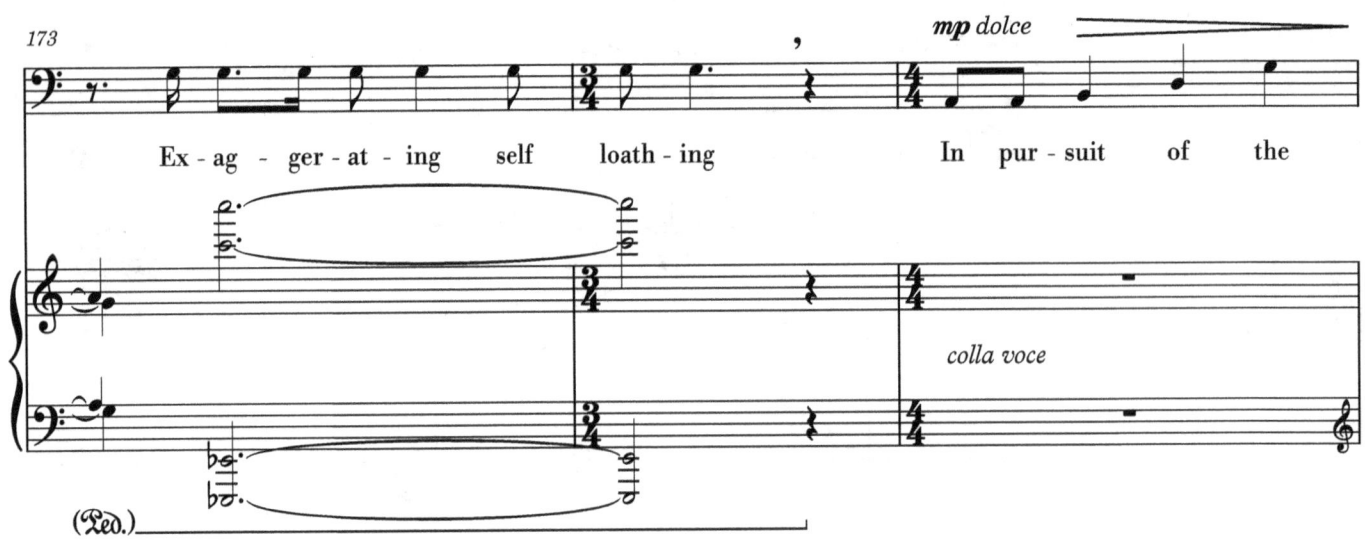

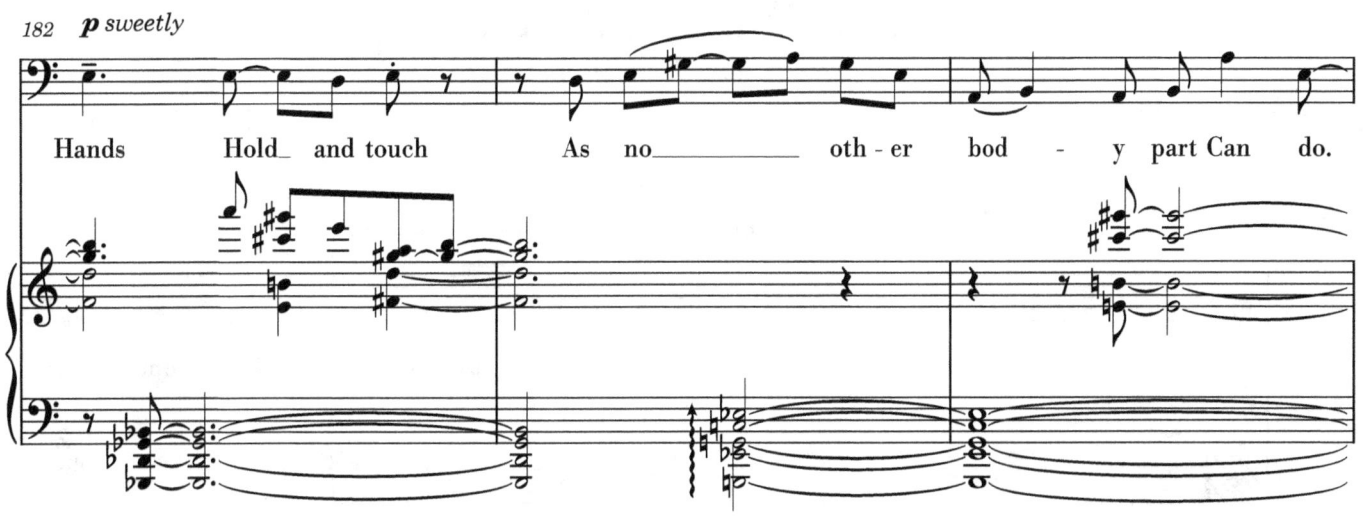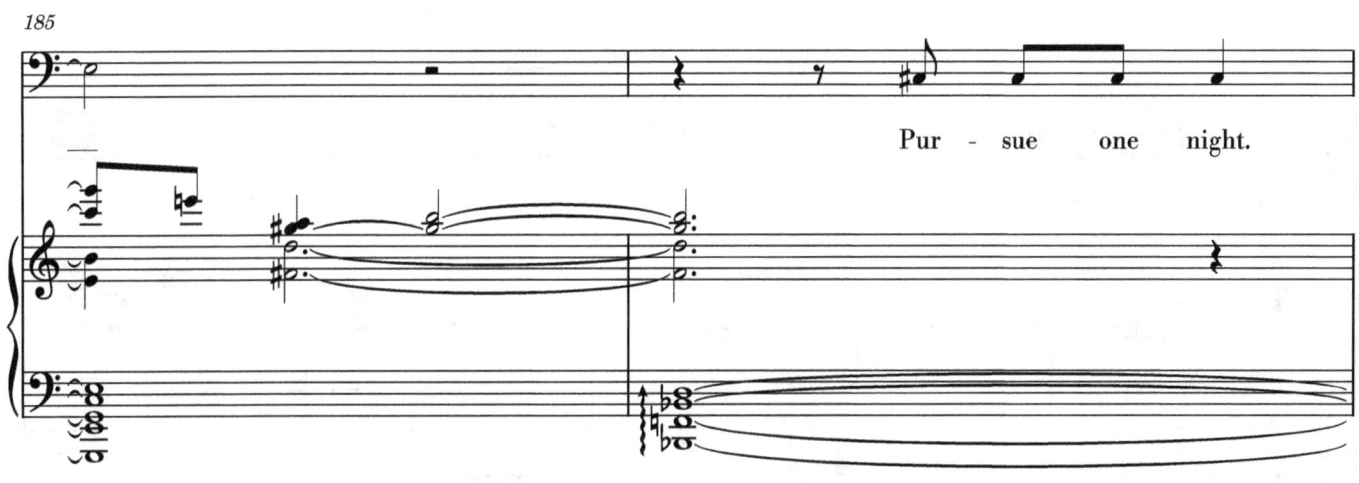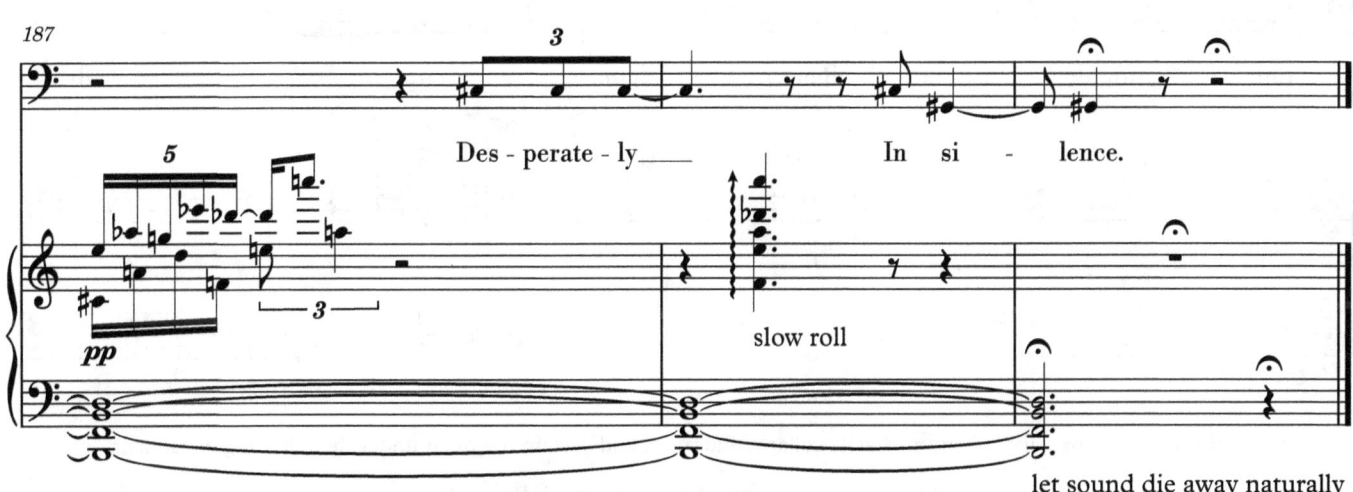

Rum Tum Tiddy-Um
from Blooms Remembered

CARL SANDBURG

PHILIP WHARTON
(2011)

* with underlined words (or syllables), immediately collapse the vowel and sustain the pitch under the following consonant.

Copyright © 2011 Nightingale Music Works. All Rights Reserved.

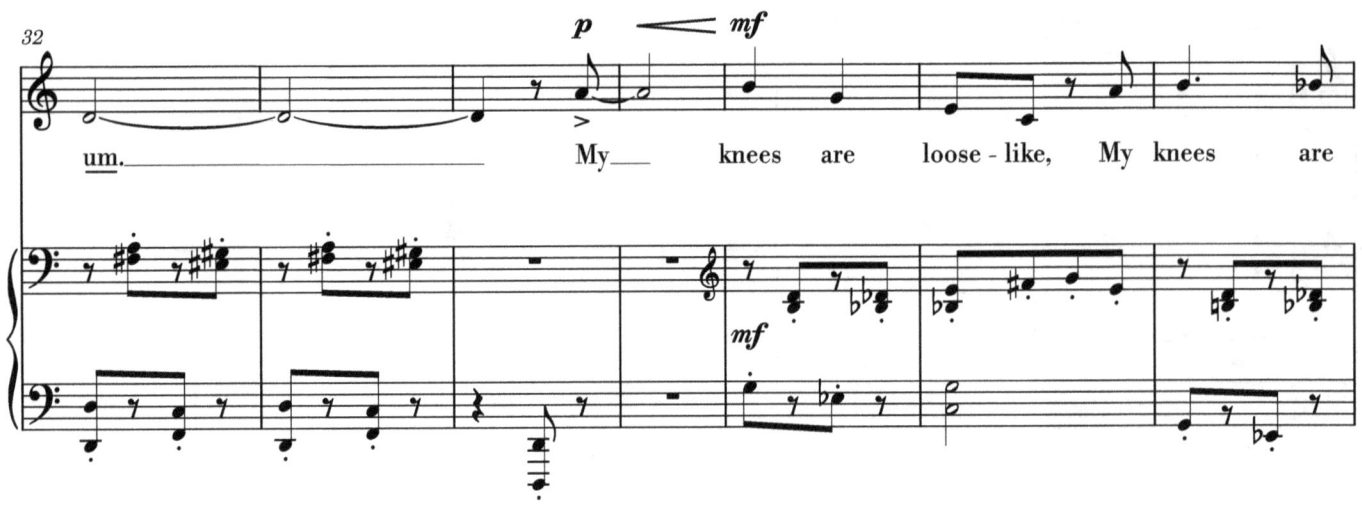

154

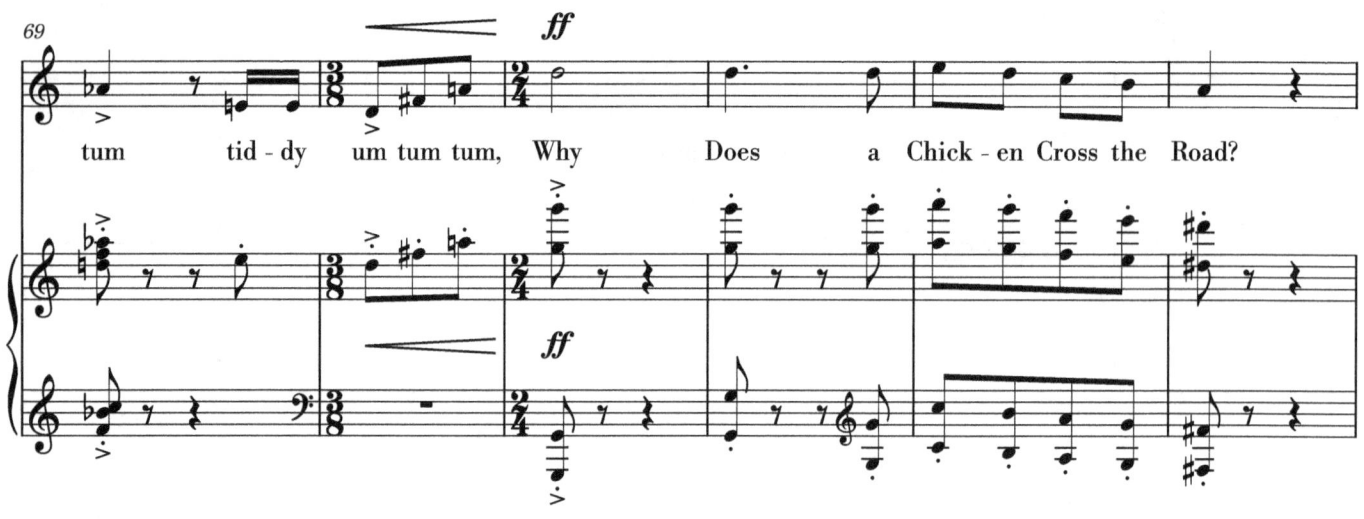

158

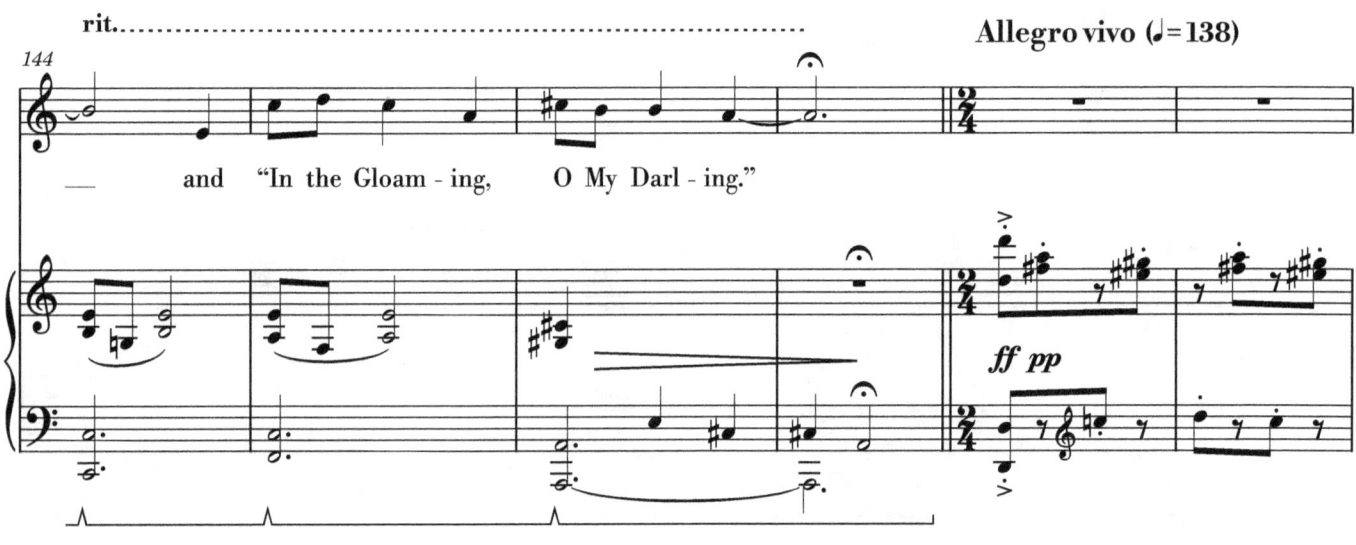

Commuter Buddhist

JEFFREY HARRISON

SCOTT WHEELER
(2014)

Copyright © 2014 Scott Wheeler Music.
Text copyright © Jeffrey Harrison. Used by permission.

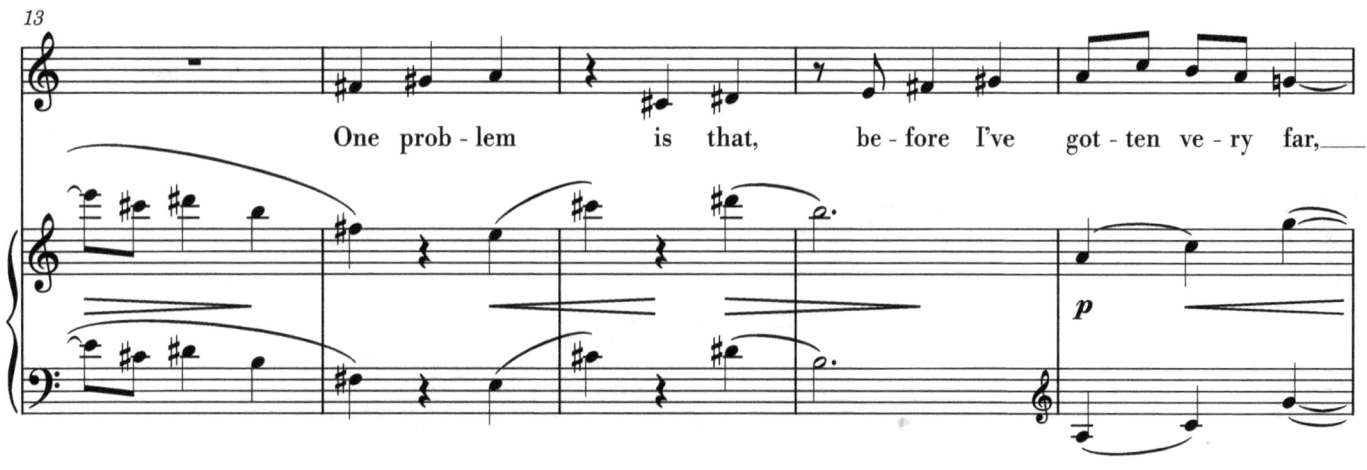
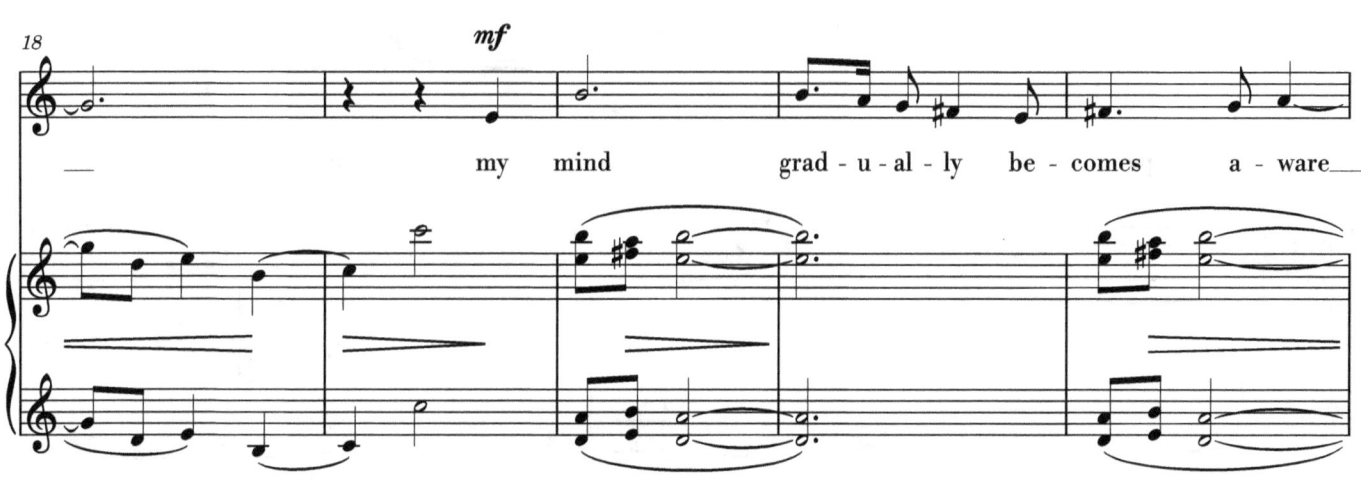

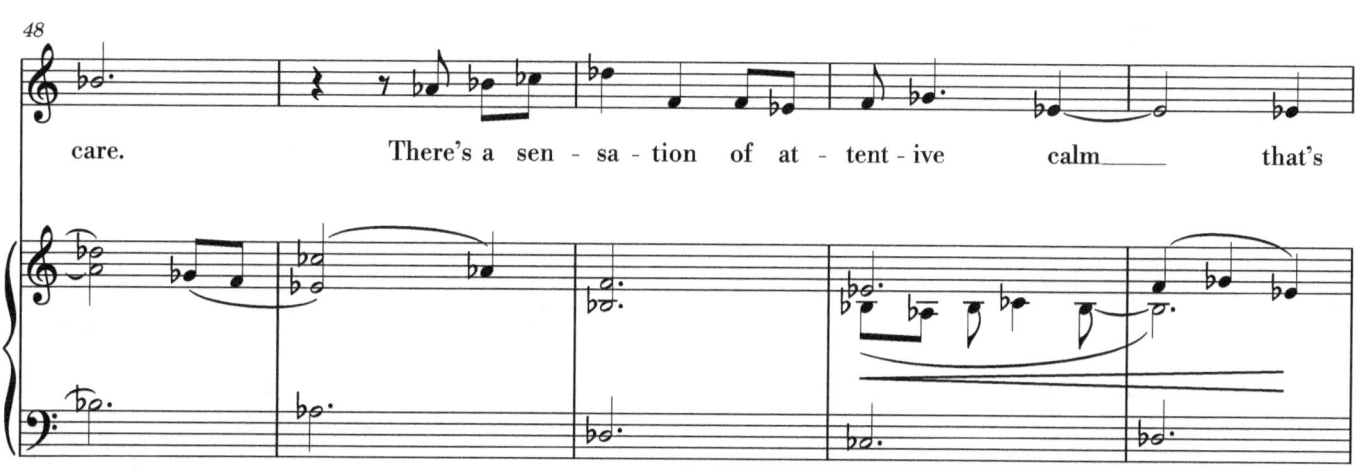

for Andy White

Pizza or Chinese
from The Ballad of Unintended Consequences

Words and music by
DAVID WOLFSON
(2015)

© 2015 Wiwo Music. All Rights Reserved.

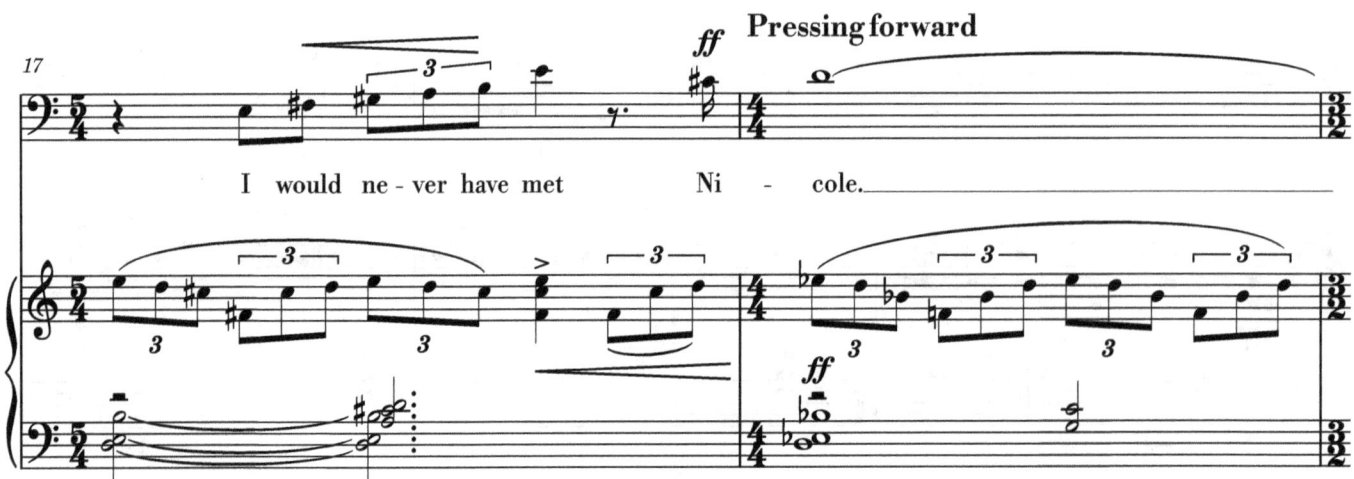

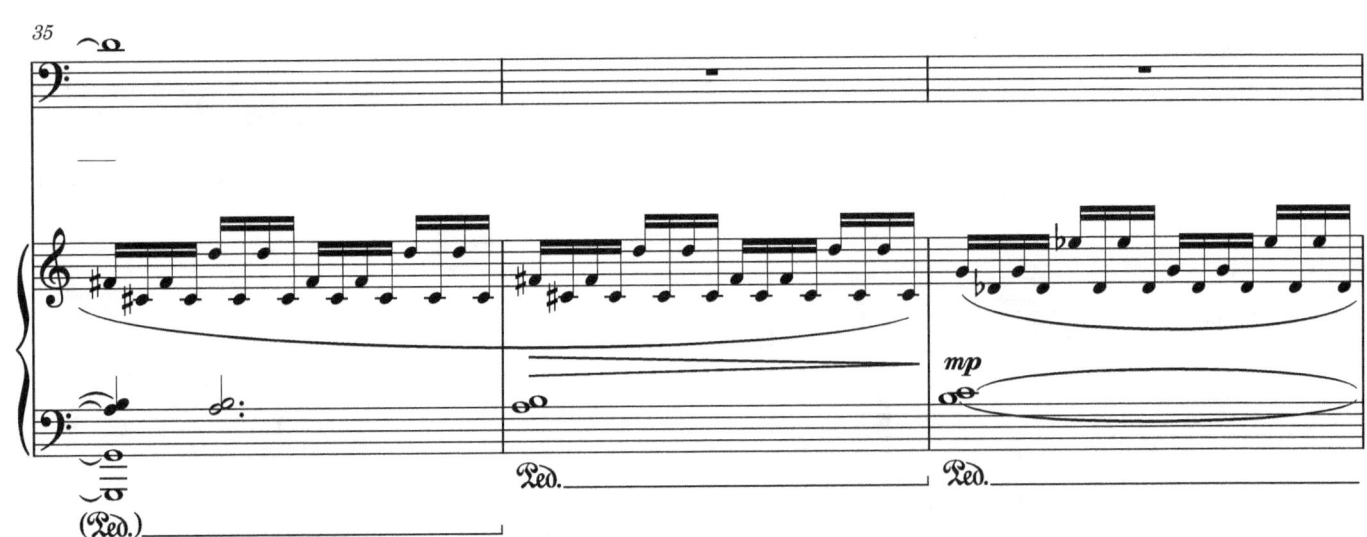

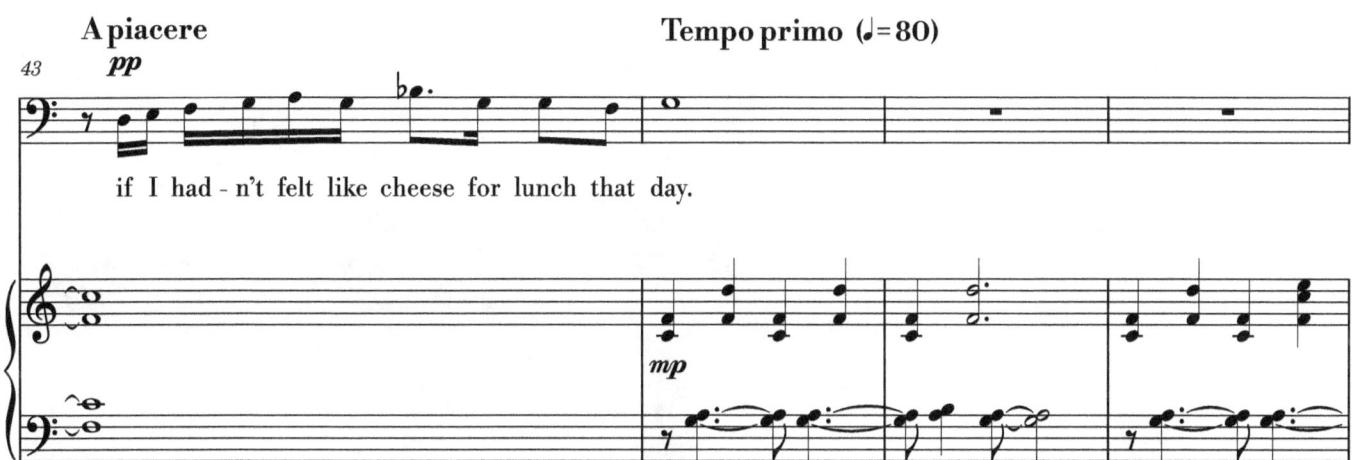

172

ABOUT THE CURATOR
Michael Kelly

www.michael-kelly.com

Praised as "expressive and dynamic" and "vocally splendid", American baritone Michael Kelly continues to distinguish himself as a consummate artist, sought-after for his riveting interpretations of recital, concert and operatic repertoire. He is a performer, educator, producer, and entrepreneur living in New York CIty.

Michael has collaborated in recital with celebrated pianists Martin Katz, Kathleen Kelly, Malcolm Martineau, Spencer Myer, Jonathan Ware and Brian Zeger. He has captivated audiences with his "exquisitely self-effacing" artistry, and is a versatile and innovative vocalist having performed with many of America's symphony orchestras and opera companies. His repertoire ranges from the baroque to modern, leading him to collaborate with some of today's most exciting composers, including Victoria Bond, Tom Cipullo, Ricky Ian Gordon, Libby Larsen, Lowell Liebermann, Reinaldo Moya, John Musto, David Sisco and Dalit Warshaw. He has performed world premiers by Matthew Aucoin, David Del Tredici, Mohammed Fairouz, and Ben Moore. Kelly is a passionate recital and chamber music interpreter, and is founder and artistic director of NY's SongFusion. He can be heard on recordings of Fairouz's *Zabur*, Del Tredici's *A Field Manual*, as well as a documentary called *Secret Music*, exploring the life and music of David Del Tredici.

Mr. Kelly has won prizes in several prominent competitions, including first prizes in 2013's Poulenc Competition and 2011's Joy in Singing. He is a graduate of The Juilliard School and the Eastman School of Music, and was a member of the Opernstudio at Opernhaus Zürich.

About the Composers

Victoria Bond (ASCAP)

b. 1945

www.victoriabond.com

A major force in 21st century music, composer Victoria Bond is known for her melodic gift and dramatic flair. Her works for orchestra, chamber ensemble and opera have been lauded by the New York Times as "powerful, stylistically varied and technically demanding."

In addition to *Soul of a Nation*, the four presidential portraits on the Albany label, highlights of Ms. Bond's catalogue include the operas *Mrs. President*, *Clara*, and *The Miracle of Light*; ballets *Equinox* and *Other Selves*; orchestral works *Thinking like a Mountain*, *Bridges*, and *Urban Bird*; and chamber works *Dreams of Flying*, *Frescoes and Ash*, and *Instruments of Revelation*, among many others. Her compositions have been performed by the New York City Opera, Shanghai, Dallas and Houston Symphonies, members of the Chicago Symphony and New York Philharmonic, American Ballet Theater and the Cassatt and Audubon Quartets.

The New York Times praised Victoria Bond's conducting as "full of energy and fervor." She has served as principal guest conductor of Chamber Opera Chicago since 2005. Prior positions include Assistant Conductor of Pittsburgh Symphony and New York City Opera and Music Director of the Roanoke Symphony and Opera, Bel Canto Opera and Harrisburg Opera. Ms. Bond has guest conducted throughout the United States, Europe, South America and Asia. She is the first woman awarded a doctorate in orchestral conducting from the Juilliard School.

Ms. Bond is Artistic Director of Cutting Edge Concerts New Music Festival in New York, which she founded in 1998, and is a frequent lecturer at the Metropolitan Opera and has lectured for the New York Philharmonic. *The Wall Street Journal*, NBC's *Today Show*, the *New York Times*, and other national publications have profiled Ms. Bond.

Martin Bussey

b. 1958

www.martinbussey.co.uk

Martin Bussey is a noted musician and educationist, combining the roles of composer, singer and conductor with his work for the Independent Schools Inspectorate. He was born in London in 1958 and educated at Haberdasher's Aske's School, Elstree before reading music as a choral scholar at King's College, Cambridge. He studied singing with John Carol Case and composition with Robin Holloway. He undertook postgraduate study at the Royal Northern College of Music.

Martin taught at Chetham's School of Music from 1988 to 2013, including as Head of Music in the Curriculum and Director of Choirs, performing on disc and at the BBC Proms. Martin sings with and directs The BBC Daily Service Singers, and is a vocal tutor at The University of Manchester.

Martin is an experienced and versatile composer with a varied catalogue of works. His interests include song, choral music for a variety of forces, and organ music, as well as instrumental works. His larger scale choral works have been well received, beginning with *The Pied Piper* (1985) and *A Brand Plucked from the Burning* (1989), his cantata celebrating the life and work of John Wesley. There have been many performances of his song cycles setting individual poets: *A Chainless Soul* (Emily Bronte), *Poems of 1912/13* (Thomas Hardy) and *Blue Remembered Hills* (A E Housman). His choral music includes challenging a capella works, such as *Ave Maria* and *Christ is the Morning Star*, as well as simpler, accompanied music, for example, *Listen Sweet Dove* (Whitsunday). Many audiences have enjoyed his choral arrangements of classics such as *I've Got You Under My Skin*, *The Carnival is Over*, and *Sentimental Journey*.

He has a great interest in the connection between words and music, giving regular recital and lecture programmes focussing on settings of individual poets (Housman, Hardy and Gurney) and the output of English song composers in general. In this capacity he is chairman of the Finzi Friends committee where he is active in promoting workshops for young performers and composers.

D. Edward Davis (BMI)

b. 1980

eddie@warmsilence.org
sound.warmsilence.org

D. Edward Davis is a composer whose work engages with the sounds of the environment, exploring processes, patterns, and systems inspired by nature.

His pieces have recently been presented at the Third Practice Electroacoustic Music Festival in Richmond, VA (2017), the EcoSono Environmental Music and Sound Art Festival in Anchorage, AK (2017), SlowSD – Festival of Slow Music in San Diego (2017), and the Clark Art Institute in Williamstown, MA (2016). His work has been performed by F-PLUS, earspace ensemble, Polyorchard, [Switch~ Ensemble], trombonist William Lang, flutist Philip Snyder, violinist Erik Carlson, Verdant Vibes, the New Mexico Contemporary Ensemble, The Witches duo, Occasional Symphony, No Exit New Music Ensemble, Musica Nova, Callithumpian Consort, the Williams College Percussion Ensemble, Soundry Ensemble, and many others.

Davis holds degrees in composition from Duke University, Brooklyn College, and Northwestern University. His former teachers include Antoine Beuger, John Supko, Amnon Wolman, David Grubbs, Amy Williams, and Michael Pisaro. Davis currently lives in New Haven, CT, where he teaches at the University of New Haven.

Twitter: @warmsilence
Soundcloud: warmsilence

Daniel Felsenfeld (ASCAP)

b. 1970

www.daniel-felsenfeld.com

Composer Daniel Felsenfeld has been commissioned and performed by Simone Dinnerstein, Opera On Tap, UrbanArias, Metropolis Ensemble, The Crossing/ICE, Meerenai Shim, the New York Philharmonic New Music Biennial, NANOWorks Opera, Kathleen Supovè, ASCAP, San Jose Opera, ETHEL, Great Noise Ensemble, American Opera Projects, the Da Capo Chamber Players, Cadillac Moon Ensemble, Nadia Sirota, and New York City Opera (VOX), and as part of the BEAT Festival, MATA Festival, Make Music New York, Ecstatic Music Festival, Opera Grows in Brooklyn, and John Wesley Harding's Cabinet of Wonders. When rapper Jay-Z performed in Carnegie Hall, along with Alicia Keys and Nas, backed by a full orchestra, Felsenfeld was asked to do all of the orchestrations and arrangements. He also collaborated with The Roots (offering music on their Grammy-nominated record Undun, appearing with them and the Metropolis Ensemble on the Jimmy Fallon Show) and ?uestlove with Keren Ann and David Murray. He also wrote arrangements for noth ShuffleCulture and Electronium, shows at the Brooklyn Academy of Music with ?uestlove, Sasha Grey, Deerhoof, Reggie Watts, and How to Dress Well and the Metropolis Ensemble. He is also the Court Composer for John Wesley Harding's Cabinet of Wonders, for which he wrote the theme—and which can be heard as an NPR Podcast. Residencies include Yaddo, the MacDowell Colony, The Hermitage, and the Atlantic Center for the Arts.

Felsenfeld is also an accomplished essayist, annotator, and author, with eight books to his name as well as articles for the New York Times, Listen, Playbill, Time Out New York, Symphony Magazine, Strings Magazine, NewMusicBox, and Early Music Magazine; program notes for the Metropolitan Opera, New York City Opera, Philadelphia Orchestra, Miller Theatre, Wigmore Hall, and Carnegie Hall; liner notes for Naxos, Bridge, Koch, EMI, Sony, and Adjustable Music. He served as curator for The Score in the Opinionator Section of the New York Times, he co-founded the New Music Gathering (an annual conference-concert series hybrid) which took place in San Francisco in 2015, as well as for Music After, a marathon concert on 9.11.11 he co-produced with Eleonor Sandresky. He is a teaching artist at the New York Philharmonic's Very Young Composers program, and lives in Brooklyn with his wife and daughter.

Cara Haxo (ASCAP)

b. 1991

chaxo91@gmail.com
www.chaxomusic.com

As a child, Cara Haxo (b. 1991) loved listening to stories read out loud. Today, she incorporates these stories, poetry, and artwork into her music. Haxo was awarded the 2013 National Federation of Music Clubs Young Composers Award, the 2013 International Alliance for Women in Music Ellen Taaffe Zwilich Prize, and second prize in the 2012 Ohio Federation of Music Clubs Student/Collegiate Composers Contest. She has been commissioned by the International Contemporary Ensemble, Quince Contemporary Vocal Ensemble, Splinter Reeds, and the PRISM Quartet, amongst other ensembles.

A native of Massachusetts, Haxo earned her Bachelors of Music in Composition at The College of Wooster, where she studied with Jack Gallagher and Peter Mowrey, and her Masters of Music in Composition at Butler University, where she studied with Michael Schelle and Frank Felice. Before Wooster, Haxo spent six summers studying at The Walden School Young Musicians Program in New Hampshire, where she has returned as faculty in recent years, teaching classes in composition, theory, and graphic notation. An avid Francophile, Haxo studied film, literature, and archeology at The Institute for American Universities in Aix-en-Provence, France, during the summer of 2011. Haxo is a doctoral candidate in composition at the University of Oregon, where she studies with Robert Kyr and David Crumb and works as a Graduate Teaching Fellow in Music Theory.

Chia-Yu Hsu (ASCAP)

b. 1975

musique123@aol.com
www.chiayuhsu.com

Born in Banqiao, Taiwan, Chiayu is an associate professor of composition at UW-Eau Claire.

She was the winner of Lakond prize from the American Academy of Arts and Letters, Left Coast Chamber Ensemble composition contest, grand prize from Symphony Number One, Suzanne and Lee Ettelson Composer's Awards, 2016 and 2013 IAWM Search for New Music, Copland House Award, Lynn University international call for scores, the 2010 Sorel Organization recording grant, music+culture 2009 International Competition for Composers, the Sorel Organization's 2nd International Composition Competition, the 7th USA International Harp Composition Competition, ASCAP Morton Gould Young Composer's Awards, the Maxfield Parrish Composition Contest, the Renée B. Fisher Foundation Composer Awards among others.

Her work has been performed by the London Sinfonietta, the Detroit Symphony Orchestra, the San Francisco Symphony, the Nashville Symphony, the Toledo Symphony, the American Composers Orchestra, the Cabrillo Festival Orchestra, the Flagstaff Symphony Orchestra, the Lynn Philharmonia Orchestra, the National Symphony Orchestra in Taiwan, Aspen Music Festival Contemporary Ensemble, Eighth Blackbird, Ciompi Quartet, and Prism Quartet.

She has received her Ph.D. at Duke University, Master of Music at Yale University School of Music, and Bachelor of Music at the Curtis Institute of Music.

Twitter: @musik123
Facebook: www.facebook.com/chiayu.hsu.39948

David Leisner (BMI)

b. 1953

leisnerdavid@gmail.com
www.davidleisner.com

David Leisner maintains a triple career as guitarist, composer and teacher. Vocal music has played a central role in his composition catalog, which otherwise includes orchestral and chamber works.

The Boston Globe's Richard Dyer wrote, "He shows imagination and taste in taking poems from disparate sources and putting them into cycles that trace emotional progress and develop dramatic shape. His prosody is excellent, and he sets words with an ear for sound, rhythm and sense…Best of all, Leisner has a gift for eloquently shaping a vocal line that is also grateful to sing." His catalog includes song sets and cycles for voice and piano - *Confiding, To Sleep, O Love is the Crooked Thing* – voice and guitar – *Confiding, Three James Tate Songs, Outdoor Shadows, West Wind, Simple Songs, Eve's Diary, Heaven's River, Five Songs of Devotion, Four Yiddish Songs - Fidelity* (tenor/soprano, baritone and piano), *Of Darkness and Light* (tenor, violin, oboe and piano), *A Timeless Procession* (baritone and string quartet), *Das Wunderbare Wesen* (baritone and cello).

His vocal music has been sung by such eminent artists as Sanford Sylvan, Wolfgang Holzmair, Kurt Ollmann, Michael Kelly, Thomas Meglioranza, Robert Osborne, Patrick Mason, Rufus Müller, William Ferguson, Paul Sperry, Andrew Fuchs, James Onstad, Dennis Tobenski, Carole Farley, Devony Smith, Juliana Gondek, Susan Narucki, Trudy Craney, D'Anna Fortunato, and Heather Johnson.

His works are published by Theodore Presser Co., G. Schirmer, Doberman-Yppan and Columbia Music. A graduate of Wesleyan University, he studied composition with Richard Winslow, Virgil Thomson, Charles Turner and David Del Tredici.

Carrie Magin (ASCAP)

b. 1981

www.carriemagin.com

With music of luminous vocal resonance, percussive intensity, and shimmering instrumentation, internationally-performed composer Carrie Magin traverses a wide emotional range with her fresh and universal voice.

Her current interests revolve around the relationship between text (sung or spoken) and music, with commissions by Georgia College Choral Ensembles, University of Cincinnati CCM Chorale, UC Women's Chorus, The Cincinnati Review, bass trombonist Russ Zokaites, and the Immanuel Presbyterian Choir in Cincinnati, OH. Recent performances include the premiere of her choral work "Heart-Fire" in Carnegie Hall in 2018 and the performance of her mini-opera "Voice on the Wire" by Boston Opera Collaborative in 2017.

Additional honors include a Fulbright Teaching Assistantship, two Art Education Grants from the New York State Council on the Arts, a Strategic Opportunity Stipend from the New York Foundation for the Arts, and composer residencies with Georgia Institute of Technology, Minnesota State University Moorhead, and Chamber Music Campania in Foggia, Italy.

Carrie Magin holds degrees from the University of Michigan and the University of Cincinnati College-Conservatory of Music. She is a member of the composition faculty at Interlochen Arts Camp, and she is currently Assistant Professor of Composition and Theory at Houghton College, where she was nominated for the Excellence in Teaching Award in 2017.

Allen McCullough

b. 1978

allenmccullough@gmail.com
www.societyofcomposers.org/members/AllenMcCullough

Dr. Allen McCullough, b.1978, is an award-winning composer currently on the music faculty at Purdue University in West Lafayette, IN.

He has composed extensively for the piano, for voice, and has several entries in the string quartet genre; he has also written for full orchestra – he has composed both a concerto for piano and orchestra, and a symphony in five movements. He has been commissioned by Chamber Music Yellow Springs, the Eakins Vocal Consort of Philadelphia, and the Lotte Lehman Foundation; he has procured grants from the Indiana Arts Commission and the National Endowment for the Arts, among other organizations.

He has collaborated with internationally recognized artists and ensembles, including Yekwon Sunwoo – pianist and 2017 Van Cliburn gold medalist, Josef Spacek – violin soloist and concertmaster of the Czech Philharmonic Orchestra, the Aeolus and Harlem String Quartets, among others.

He has earned three post-graduate degrees in musical composition, with his terminal degree (Ph.D.) in composition from the University of Pennsylvania.

Ryan Molloy (IMRO)

b. 1983

ryanmolloymusic@gmail.com
www.ryanmolloy.ie

Reflecting his innovative performances, Ryan Molloy's compositional work sits at the boundary of contemporary music and traditional Irish music. Ryan's music has been performed to international audiences on four continents for over fifteen years, including major concert venues such as Lucerne Hall, KKL (CH), Kölner Philharmonie (DE), National Concert Hall (IE), Holywell Music Room (UK) and Ulster Hall (NI). In great demand as an accompanist, he has recorded over a dozen albums and his repertoire spans numerous genres from genres from traditional Irish music to contemporary classical music, performing with the Chieftains, David Munnelly Band, Beoga, Hard Rain SoloistEnsemble, the Ulster Orchestra and the Irish Concertina Ensemble amongst others. Currently a lecturer in composition at Maynooth University, Ryan studied at the University of Oxford and latterly at Queen's University Belfast where he completed his PhD 'The Traditional Contemporary Dichotomy in Irish Art Music: A New Compositional Approach' under the supervision of Dr Simon Mawhinney and Prof. Piers Hellawell.

Ryan's compositional work has won numerous prizes and has been broadcast both nationally and internationally on BBC Radio 3 and Radio Ulster, RTÉ Lyric FM, Radio 1 and Ráidió na Gaeltachta as well as on BBC 2, UTV and BBC World. Several of Ryan's works have been chosen to represent Ireland by the International Society for Contemporary Music, at the ISCM Musicarama in Hong Kong in 2015 and at the ISCM World New Music Day in Vancouver in 2017. From 2012 to 2014, Ryan's compositional work was supported by a BBC Performing Arts Fund Fellowship in association with Moving on Music.

Facebook: @ryanmolloycomposer
Twitter: @RMolloyNUIM
Soundcloud: soundcloud.com/ryanmolloy

Ben Moore (ASCAP)

b. 1960

www.mooreart.com

The music of American composer Ben Moore includes art song, opera, musical theatre, cabaret, chamber music, choral music and comedy material. His work has been called "brilliant" and "gorgeously lyrical" by *The New York Times*, while *Opera News* has praised the "easy tunefulness" and "romantic sweep" of his songs. Singers who have performed his work include Deborah Voigt, Susan Graham, Frederica von Stade, Isabel Leonard, Lawrence Brownlee, Robert White, Nathan Gunn and Audra McDonald.

Moore composed the scores for three operas including *Enemies, a Love Story* which premiered at Palm Beach Opera in 2015. Based on the novel by Isaac Bashevis Singer, with a libretto by Nahma Sandrow, the opera has been called "an important new work that will find its place among those works that audiences will be moved by..." (Fred Plotkin/WQXR). *Odyssey* and *Robin Hood* are youth operas commissioned by the Glimmerglass Festival with librettos by Kelley Rourke. *Odyssey* premiered at Glimmerglass in 2015 and has since been seen at the Metropolitan Museum of Art and Minnesota Opera. *Opera News* called it "an opera for all ages" with an "ebullient and lyrical" score. *Robin Hood* premiered at Glimmerglass in August 2017, was seen at Seattle Opera in February 2018.

Ben's songs can be heard on Deborah Voigt's *All My Heart* (EMI) with eight Moore works, Nathan Gunn's *Just Before Sunrise* (SonyBMG), Lawrence Brownlee's *This Heart that Flutters* (Opus Arte), and *Susan Graham at Carnegie Hall* (Warner Classics). *Dear Theo* (Delos records) features three of Ben's song cycles. These include *Dear Theo*, based on the letters of Vincent van Gogh; *So Free Am I*, on poems by women; and *Ode to a Nightingale*, a setting of John Keats' great poem.

Born on January 2, 1960, in Syracuse, New York, Moore grew up in Clinton, New York and graduated from Hamilton College. With an MFA from The Parsons School of Design, Ben also pursues a career as a painter.

Gabrielle Rosse Owens (ASCAP)

b. 1982

owens.gabrielle@gmail.com
www.soundcloud.com/gabrielle_owens

Gabrielle Rosse Owens is an award-winning composer of music for orchestra, chorus and chamber ensemble. Orchestral works include *When Evening Comes* (2017) and *Royal Diadem* (2017), recorded with the UCLA Philharmonia in 2018. Recent chamber works include *The Tell-Tale Heart* (2018), written for the Moscow Contemporary Music Ensemble; *Homeward Flight* (2018), written for Armen Ksajikian, associate principal cellist with the Los Angeles Chamber Orchestra; *Balancing Act*, performed by pianist José Menor; and *Three Folk Songs* (2016), winner of the Boston New Music Initiative's 2017 Call for Scores. Upcoming projects include *The Prophecy of Daniel* (2018), a one act monodrama in three scenes with soprano Hila Plitmann and the Lyris Quartet. Honors and awards include the Elaine Krown Klein Award, the Deglin Award, President's Scholar, Phi Beta Kappa, and full scholarships to the Sorbonne University, Temple University and UCLA. She is currently pursuing doctoral studies in composition at UCLA.

Paul Salerni (BMI)

b. 1951

paul.salerni@gmail.com
www.paulsalerni.com

Paul Salerni's music has been described by *The New York Times* as "impressive" and "playful." Henry Fogel has said "It is…music that sings and dances"

Salerni's numerous commissioned orchestral and chamber music works have been performed throughout the US, Canada, Europe and China. Salerni's one-act opera *Tony Caruso's Final Broadcast* won the NOA's Chamber Opera competition in 2007, and a definitive recording of the opera was released on Naxos. His second one-act, *The Life and Love of Joe Coogan*, is an adaptation of a Dick Van Dyke TV Show episode. His new one-act dance opera on a text by Dana Gioia (*Haunted*) will be premiered in 2019. He is also in the midst of posting a YouTube video of one of his art songs each week for a year (Paul's Song of the Week).

Two CDs of Salerni's chamber music (*Touched* and *Speaking of Love*) can be found on Albany Records. His compositions are published by Presser, Alfred, Berben, and Fischer. Salerni is the NEH Distinguished Chair in the Humanities and Professor of Music. He was the recipient of Lehigh's Stabler Award for excellence in teaching and served for seven years on the Board of Directors of the Suzuki Association of the Americas, including two years as its Chair.

Harry Stafylakis (ASCAP/SOCAN)

b. 1982

info@hstafylakis.com
www.hstafylakis.com

New York City-based composer Harry Stafylakis (b. 1982) hails from Montreal, Canada. "Dreamy yet rhythmic" (*NY Times*), with a "terrible luminosity" and "ferociously expressive" (*Times Colonist*), his concert music is "an amalgamation of the classical music tradition and the soul and grime of heavy metal" (*I Care If You Listen*).

Stafylakis is the Winnipeg Symphony Orchestra's Composer-In-Residence and Festival Director & Co-Curator of the WSO's Winnipeg New Music Festival. His works have been performed by the Toronto, Winnipeg, Vancouver, Edmonton, Victoria, and FSU symphonies, American Composers Orchestra, McGill Chamber Orchestra, ICE, Contemporaneous, Mivos Quartet, Aspen Contemporary Ensemble, Nouveau Classical Project, mise-en, Lorelei Ensemble, and American Modern Ensemble. He has been featured at the NY Philharmonic Biennial, Aspen Music Festival, Winnipeg New Music Festival, and the Montreal International Classical Guitar Festival.

Awards include the Charles Ives Fellowship from the American Academy of Arts and Letters, the ASCAP Foundation's Leonard Bernstein Award, four SOCAN Foundation Awards for Young Composers, and grants from the Canada Council for the Arts, NYSCA, and New Music USA. He serves on the board of directors of GroundSwell (Winnipeg) and the interdisciplinary curatorial panel of I-Park Foundation (CT), is an Associate Composer of the Canadian Music Centre, and a founding member of the NYC composer collective ICEBERG New Music.

Upcoming projects include new works for the Winnipeg and Ottawa symphonies, Roomful of Teeth, Hard Rubber Orchestra, Contemporaneous, Periapsis Music and Dance, Cowan–Cicchillitti guitar duo, and pianist Jenny Lin. In 2018–19, he will also be collaborating with progressive metal pioneers Animals As Leaders on adaptations of their music for metal band & orchestra.

Stafylakis holds degrees from McGill University and The Graduate Center, CUNY, and lectures at the City College of New York.

Margaret Tesch-Muller

www.margaretteschmuller.com

Australian-born Margaret Tesch-Muller is an internationally-performed composer, conductor and soprano currently working in the United States. With intriguing harmonies and lyrical lines, her compositions deeply touch both performers and audiences alike. Her latest commission, a song cycle entitled *Voices of a Northern Year*, was premiered at the Sydney Opera House by the Hourglass Ensemble.

Margaret's innate interest in people, combined with an excellent knowledge of the voice and a unique ability to communicate the shape and emotion of music has led to her becoming a sought-after guest conductor. She has worked extensively with children's, community, school and church choirs for many years, including The Australian Girls' Choir, The Queensland Show Choir, Choirbolical and the St Peter's Lutheran Church Choir of Indooroopilly.

Her lyric soprano voice has been described as soothing and beautiful. She has been a soloist on various occasions including at the Brighton Festival Fringe and has extensive cantoring and choral experience.

Margaret holds a Bachelor of Music with Honours in Vocal Performance from the University of Queensland, with secondary studies in composition and conducting, and a Bachelor of Arts in Studies of Religion. She has also worked as a Vocal and Piano coach and Adjudicator.

Craig Urquhart (ASCAP)

b. 1953

www.craigurquhart.com

The music of composer/pianist Craig Urquhart is a continuing renewal of faith in beauty and the healing power of music.

Craig continues on his musical path with his latest CD release *Calm Seas*. *Calm Seas* is Craig's ninth solo piano album. His previous acclaimed albums are: *First Light*, *Within Memory*, *Secret Spaces*, *Streamwalker*, *Evocation*, *Songs Without Words*, *The Dream of the Ancient Ones*, and *Epitaphs and Portraits*.

Craig has performed throughout the United States, and has also toured in Japan, Italy, Germany, France and Belgium. Craig continues to share his music in new and various ways. He supplied many solo piano works for the soundtrack to the 2010 Teddy Award Winning (Berlinale) film *Postcards To Daddy*.

Craig contributed the first movement of a secular Requiem based on the words of poet Jackie Kay, commissioned for World AIDS Day to benefit Mission Malawi.: *The Moon, My Man and I*. The Halle Orchestra and Chorus premiered this work conducted by Sir Mark Elder, CBE with soloists Roderick Williams and Rebecca Bottone.

His album of his songs, *Secret and Divine Signs* with tenor Michael Slattery received Five Star ratings from the *BBC Music Magazine* and *FM Classic Music Magazine*. Andrew Stewart in *FM Classic Music Magazine* wrote: "... the songs of Urquhart, with their seamless tonal melodies and rippling keyboard accompaniments ... transport the listener into a state of tranquil contemplation by Slattery's sincere delivery."

In reviewing *Calm Seas*, Kathy Parsons for MainlyPiano.com wrote: " I defy anyone to duplicate the soulful, honest, and heartfelt expression Urquhart pours into every note and chord. That's where the magic lies ... you come away feeling that you have gotten to know him rather well - and have perhaps also seen a new facet of your own soul.. it is always a very special experience to be reminded of the power of quiet beauty and simplicity. "

Mark Lanz Weiser (ASCAP)

b. 1968

marklanzweiser@gmail.com
www.marklanzweiser.com

Mark Lanz Weiser is a composer of opera and concert music. His music has been described as "brilliantly expressive" (*Washington Post*), "potent and well-made" (*San Francisco Chronicle*), and "ravishing" (*San Jose Mercury News*). Awards include the ASCAP Foundation Rudolf Nissim Prize, the Ithaca College International Heckscher Composition Prize, and the NATS National Art Song competition. He has held residencies at the Yaddo colony in New York and the Virginia Center for the Creative Arts and his music has been published by Boosey & Hawkes and Editions Bim International Music Publishing.

Mark Lanz Weiser received his bachelor's degree in piano performance and master's degree in composition from the Peabody Conservatory of the Johns Hopkins University. He is currently Assistant Professor in Composition and Director of Music Theory at the University of Southern California's Thornton School of Music.

Philip Wharton (ASCAP)

b. 1969

pdwharton@gmail.com
www.philipwharton.com

Few artists enjoy such high praise for both of their disciplines as composer/violinist PHILIP WHARTON. Of his playing, *The New York Times* proclaimed, "a rousing performance!" and *The Waterloo Courier* wrote, "a golden tone with breathtaking execution." His compositions, heralded from coast to coast, are described by the *New York Concert Review* as, "…decidedly contemporary…both engaging and accessible." Writing from symphony to song, past seasons saw the Santa Fe Opera's remounting of *Two Saintes Caught in the Same Act* as part of their apprentice scenes program, the Grammy-nominated Borealis Wind Quintet perform his *Quintet* on their concert tours, his chamber symphony, *Passing Season* performed by regional orchestras, premiere of his *Symphony*, his tribute to Shakespeare's 450th birthday, a song cycle entitled *Fools*, and concerts with Grammy-nominated soprano, Caroline Worra. Other projects include collaborations with author Janet Burroway and illustrator John Vernon Lord to create musical settings of their books for children: *The Giant Jam Sandwich*, *The Truck on the Track*, and a vocal-monodrama, *The Perfect Pig*. Recent recordings include Albany Records' release of his *Flute Sonata*—performed by flutist, Katherine Fink, and pianist Rose Grace, Crescent Phase Records' release of his *Woodwind Quintet*—performed by the Madera Woodwind Quintet, and Kenneth Thompkins' (principal Detroit Symphony Orchestra) recording of his *Alto-Trombone Sonata*. Expect to see the release of a CD by Elizabeth Sombart with the Royal Philharmonic Orchestra in the coming year.

Scott Wheeler (ASCAP)

b. 1952

scott_wheeler@emerson.edu
www.scottwheeler.org

Scott Wheeler's most recent opera is *Naga*, on a libretto of Cerise Jacobs, co-commissioned by White Snake Projects and Boston Lyric Opera. Scott's previous operas have been commissioned by the Metropolitan Opera/Lincoln Center Theatre, Washington National Opera and the Guggenheim Foundation. Scott's 2017 violin sonata, *The Singing Turk*, was commissioned and premiered by Sharan Leventhal, and has been performed many times around the world by Gil Shaham and Akira Eguchi. Other recent works include *200 Dreams from Captivity* for baritone and orchestra on texts of Wang Dan, *Ben Gunn* on texts of Paul Muldoon, and *Nightingale*, a new narrative ballet with choreographer Melissa Barak.

Scott's most recent CDs include *Portraits and Tributes*, featuring pianist Donald Berman, on Bridge, and *Songs to Fill the Void*, featuring baritone Robert Barefield and pianist Carolyn Hague, on Albany. Other Wheeler CDs include *Crazy Weather*, with the Boston Modern Orchestra Project conducted by Gil Rose, *Wasting the Night* -- songs for voice and piano, and the opera *The Construction of Boston*, both available on Naxos; *Shadow Bands* features Scott's chamber music for strings and piano with the Gramercy Trio, recorded on Newport Classic. Scott Wheeler is Senior Distinguished Artist in Residence at Emerson College in Boston, where he teaches musical theatre and songwriting.

Facebook: www.facebook.com/scott.wheeler.52035

David Wolfson (ASCAP)

b. 1964

david@davidwolfsonmusic.net
www.davidwolfsonmusic.net

David Wolfson holds a PhD in composition from Rutgers University, and has taught at Rutgers University, Montclair State University and Hunter College. He is enjoying an eclectic career, having composed opera, musical theatre, touring children's musicals, and incidental music for plays; choral music, band music, orchestral music, chamber music, art songs, and music for solo piano; comedy songs, cabaret songs and one memorable score for an amusement park big-headed-costumed-character show. His CD *Seventeen Windows*, featuring the solo piano suite *Seventeen Windows* and the *Sonata for Cello and Piano*, is available from Albany Records, iTunes and Amazon.com. For more information: www.davidwolfsonmusic.net.

Facebook: www.facebook.com/davidwolfsonmusic/

Supplementary Materials

Texts, program notes, composer biographies, and composer headshots can be found at:

https://newmusicshelf.com/anthologies/baritone-v1-info/